STILL FULL

When God Breaks Your Heart

By

Loretta Paige

ISBN: 979-8-9929985-0-4

Published by:
M. L. Paige

Edited by:
Spirit of Excellence Writing & Editing Services, LLC
www.TakeUpThySword.com

Contents

Introduction

The death of a loved one evokes a myriad of emotions in us. Some of those emotions are hurt, anger, disappointment, and confusion. The bible tells us, *In everything to give thanks, for this is the will of God in Christ Jesus concerning you (1 Thessalonians 5:18).* But how do we give thanks to God when our hearts are shattered, and we are overcome with grief that seems to be unbearable? This book is about Vincent Gerard Paige Sr., the love of my life, and the perfect marriage God quickly gave us. Then what seemed to be just as quick, He took him. God strengthened me to thank Him through the tears and brokenness. While I was giving God my broken heart, He was mending it and has filled the broken places with Himself.

This book is about the twist and turns of our lives together and the sustaining love of God that was always with us even when we didn't recognize it. That love pursued us, captured us, captivated us, and then raptured us so that we could receive what He had prepared for us. There was nothing honorable about the events that started our relationship. I would even call them shameful on my part, but it is what it is. That's what makes it all the more amazing what God did in us and for us. Even in my foolishness, God's love led me to the love of my life, brought us together in marriage, transformed us in His refining fire of marital discontent, and gave us marital bliss.

Then my husband received the diagnosis of an aggressive malignant cancer and God's love held us together. He had given us firsthand experience of His healing power when He healed our daughter who was at the brink of death, so we knew that cancer was nothing for Him to heal. During the radiation and chemo, God's love strengthened us to go through the treatments thanking Him and giving Him all the praise because no matter what, He was still worthy to be praised. After several months of no detection of the cancer, it returned. My husband agreed to have his arm amputated hoping that would be the end of the cancer. Knowing my spirit was in turmoil because of his decision, I got a sign from God that gave me peace and the fortitude to go full steam ahead. Still, after my husband's arm amputation, the cancer came back again and metastasized to other parts of his body. There was nothing more the doctors could do for him and hospice was called.

God's love welcomed my breaking heart in His presence and strengthened me to watch the love of my life die from a sickness that I know He could've healed but He didn't. Instead, God allowed cancer to be the death of the phenomenal man that He favored me with, knowing that my heart would be shattered because of what He had given us. Just as much, God also knew that His love was more than enough to sustain me and mend my broken heart even in those times I did not feel like it was. This is our journey.

Chapter 1

The Beginning of Us

In the spring of 1987, I met Vincent when he came to my mom's house with my brother Tony. Tony was married to Vincent's cousin Diane. When Tony walked in, two guys walked in with him, and it was instantly noticeable that they were identical twins. My brother introduced them to my mom and those of us who were at her house as Diane's cousins, Vincent and Victor. We had a nice cordial exchange, but there were no sparks or anything of that nature; I did not think twice about Vincent or Victor for that matter. A couple of months later as I was driving into the apartment complex where my mom lived, Diane's sister, Nita, was leaving my mom's apartment and Vincent was one of the passengers in her car. I stopped to speak to Nita and the others who were in the car with her and while I was speaking, I noticed Vincent looking at me with a sparkle in his eyes and a smile on his face. He was trying to get my attention, but I was not moved by him at all. After we finished speaking and asking about each other's wellbeing, Nita drove off and I proceeded to park my car.

At the time, I had two kids, Delrick and Fantasy, and was living with their father Clarence so I was not interested in another relationship. During the time with Clarence, he had several indiscretions with other women and had even given me an STD more than once. The husband of one of those indiscretions came to our house to confront him about seeing his wife, but Clarence wasn't home so he informed me that his wife was having sex him. He went on to say that his wife admitted to having sex with him in our bed. I was upset about it, but I felt sorrier for the husband of the woman because I saw how much it hurt him. I had seen him and his wife around town, and I saw that his wife might have been a little slow in her mental faculties. When the husband came to my house and began speaking, he stuttered badly and from his speech, it seemed that he was a little slow as well.

"You ought to be ashamed of yourself; you know both of them are slow," I said to Clarence because I believed he had taken advantage of them because of their diminished mental capacity. Still, I stayed with him and remained faithful but it wasn't like I didn't have opportunities to sleep with other guys. I never cheated on him but when I learned he had been sleeping with someone I considered a friend, I was disgusted and hurt because to me, that was low down. He might as well had been with one of my sisters because that was how I thought of this young lady. I was upset, and I wanted revenge but I still did not want to leave him. I wanted to keep our family together, but I also wanted him to feel the hurt and betrayal that I felt. So I set out on a mission to find someone to have revenge sex with. I know that was foolish of me but at the time, that's what I wanted to do so that's what I did. I thought to myself, "Here I am being faithful to someone who takes my faithfulness for granted so he doesn't deserve it."

The Deluxe Bar was a popular hangout spot in my hometown of Sanford, Florida. We called it The Bar and on Sunday evenings, it was the place to be. I was not the hangout type, but I went because that's what Clarence enjoyed doing. Then I started enjoying it because it was something to do, and we usually met up with family and friends. Most people came and sat outside in the parking lot either in or on their cars. Talking, drinking, smoking, playing music, and laughing with family and friends was the atmosphere. It was a good time until a fight broke out because then it was time to scatter, at least for me.

There was one occasion when Clarence and I were sitting outside of The Bar in the car, and a car quickly approached near to where we were parked. A guy got out with a gun in his hand and walked up to my sister's boyfriend, put the gun to his head and said, "N***a, I'll kill you!" An argument ensued and they began fighting. I just knew my sister's boyfriend would be shot in the head, but he did not back down from the guy with the gun.

"Oh no, he's gonna shoot him, he's gonna shoot him!" I yelled while Clarence helped me as I crawled out of my car to get on the ground because I did not want to see my sister's boyfriend get shot. It was a harrowing experience because I had never seen anything like that before in my life. After the fight was over, the guy with the gun got back in his car and left as quickly as he came because someone had called the police. I was just thankful no one was shot or killed.

In my calculated foolishness of revenge sex, I had one stipulation: the guy could not be from Sanford. My thought was that it was just going to be a one-time thing and if he was not from the area, then maybe Clarence would not find out about it unless I told him. Vincent and Victor were born in Sanford, but they grew up in Rochester, New York. After graduating from high school in Rochester, they both moved to Daytona Beach, Florida, to attend Bethune Cookman College. Because they had family who lived in Sanford, they were there often. Incidentally, I had heard that one of them was living in and seeing a girl from Sanford and I was not trying to have sex with him because he was someone else's man.

One Sunday evening while my sister Gail and I were sitting in the car outside The Bar, I noticed one of the twins leaning against a car that was parked next to ours. "Gail, which one of those twins is that; the one that lives here or the other one?" I asked because if he was the one who lived in Sanford, I was not going to say anything to him.

"It's the other one, Lo," Gail said with certainty. Vincent was actually the one who lived in and was seeing someone from Sanford. I thought the one leaning against the car was Victor; but I was not sure who was who and obviously Gail was not sure either.

To get his attention, I said, "Hey," thinking I was speaking to the other twin. When he turned and looked at me, I asked, "Which one of the twins are you?"

He knew I was flirting with him and he answered, "Vince."

"Hey, Vince, how are you?" I asked.

"I'm fine," he answered, and then asked, "How are you?"

"Fine," I answered and that was the extent of our conversation that evening. I still did not know if he was the one who lived in Sanford or if I would ever see him again. Although I am sure he had been there, I do not recall ever seeing Vincent at The Bar before that evening. Also, with no offense to my wonderful brother-in-law whom I love dearly, I am sure glad it was Vincent who was there and not Victor. They were identical twins but their personalities were not. They both were fun-loving people, but Vincent's personality was reserved and laid-back, while Victor's was outgoing and talkative. His family said I got the "good" twin. I believe I got the "better" twin as far as a relationship is concerned. Furthermore, I believe God had Vincent there at that time for me.

Later in the week, Vincent had my sister-in-law (his cousin) call me for him. "Hello," I said as I answered the phone.

"Lo, he asked me to call you," Diane said.

"Huh?, Oh, hey, Diane," I said because Clarence was in the room when I answered the phone. I proceeded to talk extra loud on the phone in the hopes that Diane would get the hint that he was in the room, but she didn't and continued talking.

"Lo, he wants to see you," she went on to say.

"Oh, okay, Diane, I will talk to you later," I said extra loud again, still hoping she would get the hint that I could not talk but she didn't. I could not get her off the phone soon enough. Clarence was not stupid and he knew I was trying to hint at Diane that he was in the room. After I hung up the phone, he asked me what she wanted, and I made up a lie. I am sure he knew I was lying, but it did not matter to me because I had a plan and it was going to happen.

The following Sunday, I went back to The Bar with Gail and we sat in the car. Gail knew about Clarence's indiscretions and although she did not come out and say it, I knew she wanted me to see someone else, so she was all for me talking to Vincent. After Vincent and I spoke to each other at The Bar the previous Sunday and my sister-in-law called to tell me he wanted to talk to me, I knew I did not have to look any further for someone to have revenge sex with. I was glad it happened quicker than I thought it would because I was not in the habit of accosting other guys for the purpose of having sex with them. Vincent made the search easy for me because I didn't have to engage with anyone else. I had made up my mind that he was going to be the one and there he was again, chilling in the parking lot at The Bar. Earlier, I had asked my sister Star for the key to her apartment just in case I saw Vincent and we wanted to go somewhere to talk. Neither Gail nor Star knew about my plans to have revenge sex with him, but Gail knew I wanted to talk to him. She also knew we could not talk at The Bar because there was a chance Clarence could show up there.

We parked next to where Vincent was and I asked, "Hey, you want to go somewhere that we can talk?"

"Yes," he answered smiling, so he got in the car with me and we went to Star's apartment. Vincent did not know my intentions and I know he did not think we were having sex that evening.

Once inside Star's apartment, we sat on the couch and talked for a little while. I do not remember much about the conversation, but I remember him asking, "What kind of things do you like to do?" I don't remember what my answer was or even if I answered. He went on to say, "I like to go to the movies. Do you like to go to the movies?"

We chit chatted for a little but I only had one thing on my mind and getting to know him was not it. I don't think Vincent had any inkling that I wanted to have sex with him but for some reason, he took his shirt off while we were talking; I thought that was odd but I didn't mind it. We continued talking and then he held my hand, which led to us kissing. One thing led to another, and we ended up on the floor having sex. It was only for a few minutes though because Star came home and shut everything down. I believe she came home to be nosy because she knew we were there. After getting ourselves together, Vincent and I went back to The Bar and I was satisfied that I had accomplished what I had set out to do. If I did not hear from Vincent again, it would have been fine with me because it was just revenge sex. When I look back at what I did, I shake my head in utter disbelief. I have done some foolish things in my life, but that had to be somewhere near the top of the list. Not only did I seek out to have sex with someone I did not know, but he could have been a total nutcase. All I can say to that is, "Lord, thank you for watching over this fool."

That is my story of how we met, but Vincent had his own story: "Girl, I had been watching you before you said something to me at The Bar," he admitted. Vincent had a friend who lived in the same apartment complex as my mom, and he used to go play cards there. From her kitchen window, he could see who was coming to or leaving from my mama's apartment. "I saw you get out your car and I asked Diane, 'Who's that pretty red bone getting out that car?'"

"Boy, that girl don't want you; that's a good girl," is what he told me Diane said.

He told me his response was, "And I'm a good boy." He went on to say, "I told Diane you was gon be my wife; you are the wife I dreamed of, the wife I asked God for."

"Aw, boy, if I hadn't said something to you at The Bar, you wouldn't have said nothing to me," I told him.

"Yeah, I would've; I was just waiting for the right time," he said. "When I went to play cards, I made sure I sat in the chair facing the window so I could see you when you came up. If it was my turn to play a card and you were coming up, I'd be watching you so hard, they had to get my attention back to the card game. 'You gon play cards or what man?'" he said they asked. "Come on, I'm playing cards," he said. "All I needed was the chance to say something to you and when you said something to me at The Bar, that was my green light to pursue."

After our first sexual encounter, I thought, "I did it and I'm done." Vincent did not know my intentions, and I did not know he had intentions of his own. I don't know what made me think I could just have sex with a man and that would be the end of it. I thought I could do what Clarence was doing: cheat with someone and go home and continue our relationship, but it wasn't that simple for me. Vincent reached out to me through my sister-in-law, but I rejected him because I did not want a relationship with him. I did not want to leave Clarence, I just wanted to pay him back. Still, Vincent would not give up and eventually, I gave in. I agreed to see him again, again, and again. We often talked about the way we met after we had been together for a while, and I would remind him that I did not want a relationship with him. "I didn't like you like that," I would say.

"Look at you now; persistence overcomes resistance," was always his response and I agreed with him because that's what happened in our case. Our encounters were mostly sexual but the more time we spent together, the more time we wanted to spend together.

The more we talked, we discovered we had common interests. We both enjoyed listening to music, dancing, and watching sports such as basketball and football. Initially, it was about the sex but as we got to know each other, the fondness blossomed. I was still living with Clarence, so we could not see each other as often as we wanted to. We would discreetly get together about once a week.

I was working the third shift at my job and had determined that the most opportune time for me and Vincent to get together was in the morning after I got the kids off to school and Clarence went to work. Vincent was working with a moving company and the jobs he went on were out of town; so on the days he was in town, we made our plans to have our rendezvous. I would rush home from work, get the kids off to school, take a shower and then head to Sanford before sleep came down on me. My kids were in elementary school so I had about four hours to spend with him before I had to pick them up. As time went on, I felt more comfortable about going to see him and became less worried about running into Clarence.

Vincent was living with one of his friends when we first began seeing each other but when I went to see him, the friend was never home, and that is how I wanted it. However, his friend knew Vincent and I were seeing each other because whenever I saw him out, he said something about it. I didn't mind him knowing, but I didn't want him telling others so I told Vincent to make that clear to him. Sometimes when I arrived to see Vincent, he had breakfast ready for me and we would sit and eat while watching a little television before heading to the bedroom. Other times, we went straight to the bedroom because I knew I had to be home in time to pick up the kids. By the time I did get home after working all night, spending the mornings with him, picking up the kids from school and getting them fed and settled, I would be dog tired. Then with little to no sleep, I usually had to return to work that night. I worked at a factory that made hypodermic needles and I was an inspector. I don't know what kind of needles I passed because I could barely keep my eyes open to see them.

Vincent had a genuineness about him that I was not familiar with, and I was attracted to it. It was pure and it was all so fresh to me. He did not try to play games or put on a show pretending to be something or someone that he was not. After being in a relationship for seven years with someone who was full of deception and lies, it was refreshing to be with someone and just enjoy him without either one of us expecting anything from the other except to enjoy the times we were able to be together. He knew I was in a relationship, and I did not question him about whether he was in one. Nevertheless, my heart was beginning to desire Vincent. Clarence and I continued to go to The Bar on Sunday evenings, and I hoped to see Vincent out there. Sometimes, we just rode through the parking lot, and I would see him out of the corner of my eye with a big smile and winking his eye at me with his skinny sexy self. I'd smile to myself as we rode by because I did not want to give myself or Vincent away.

Eventually, Clarence learned of the sexual encounter I had with Vincent at Star's apartment. "I know you went to Star's apartment and had sex with that twin," he said.

"Yeah, I did," I responded.

"Are you still seeing him?" he asked.

"Not anymore," I answered. Surprisingly, he began crying. I had never seen him cry like that and I did not see it coming. All those times he had cheated on me with no remorse but now that it was his turn to be the one cheated on, he could not take it. I had no sympathy for his tears at all. Did he think he was the only one who could cheat in our relationship, or did he think he was the only one who would cheat? I don't know what he thought and I did not care. I lied to him when I told him I was not seeing Vincent anymore because I couldn't wait until the next time. By that time, what he said did not matter. I was doing what I wanted to do and that was to see Vincent. We continued to discreetly see each other whenever we could.

I knew Clarence had an idea that I was going to see Vincent after I left work in the mornings because he started wanting me to ride with him during the day while he was working as a truck driver. I told him I could not do it because I had to get some sleep. "You can sleep in the truck while I make my deliveries," he said.

"Okay, I'll ride with you," I said just to appease him. I tried sleeping in the truck, but it didn't work out for me because I couldn't get comfortable enough to sleep. After a couple of times, I told him I couldn't ride with him because I needed my rest.

After Vincent and I had been seeing each other for several months, he said, "I really wanna spend more time with you. I wanna do things with you like take you out and do other things with you."

"I do to, but I am still in a relationship with him," I said. Vincent and I both wanted more, but it was not my plan to leave Clarence to be with him. In my mind, Vincent was someone to have revenge sex with because I knew that Clarence was still cheating.

One night as Clarence and I were arguing about me seeing Vincent, he said, "With your slick a**," because he knew I was still seeing Vincent.

"I was taught by the best," I said sarcastically. I knew that I was not going to be with him much longer because of my feelings for Vincent.

Chapter 2

Guns and Drugs

Each time I came to Sanford, I wanted to see Vincent. Vincent had moved in with his sister Stacy and on Friday nights (which were my off nights from work), I started going to her apartment to spend time with him. But a couple of times, he was not there; and each time, Stacy told me he left with one of his friends. Vincent began spending time with a friend whom I had not met. I did not know who he was, so I was a little turned off by it and stopped seeing him for a while. After a couple of months, I saw his sister Stacy in a restaurant and she said, "You haven't been over there to see Vincent in a while."

"I know but every time I come, he's gone with his friend, so I stopped coming," I said.

"I'll tell him I saw you," she said.

"Okay," was my response.

Eventually, Vincent and I started talking and seeing each other again, and I learned that his friend was a big-time drug dealer in Sanford. I never asked him how they met but they became friends, and Vincent began selling drugs for him. When I met Vincent, he was working for a moving company but he stopped working for the moving company to sell drugs. That was in the late 1980's, and crack cocaine was rampant at that time. I was never into drug use and did not care for Vincent selling drugs; but he was just someone I was having sex with, so I didn't make a big deal of it.

One night while I was at work, I received a call from Clarence, and he said that someone had tried to break into our house, and I needed to come home. "Are you all alright?" I asked.

"Yes, but you need to come home," he said. Immediately, I left my job not knowing what was going on at my house and what to expect when I arrived there, especially with my kids. As I pulled up to the house, I was expecting to see police cars and lights. Instead, he was standing outside and came around to the passenger side of the car and got in.

"Is everything alright? Where are the kids?" I asked.

"They're inside sleep," he answered. Then he pulled out a gun. I was stunned and terrified! While pulling my underwear out of his pocket, he said, "I found your underwear in the dirty clothes; you had sex." Then he showed me that there was something in my underwear that led him to believe I had had sex. "You had sex with him tonight, didn't you?" he demanded.

"No, I didn't," I said as I began to try and get out of the car, but he would not let me.

"If you don't admit to me you had sex with him, I'll kill you," he said.

I started crying and screaming, "No I didn't have sex; so, if you gon kill me, just go ahead and kill me!" I cried. I did not know what was going on in his crazed mind. My thought was that he was on drugs or something because I had not had sex that night. It seemed like we were in the car for hours, but it was just a few minutes. I tried to scream loud enough for the neighbors to hear me, but no one heard me. After he realized that I was not going to admit I had sex while he had the gun pointed at me, he put it down and began slapping me in my face to get me to admit it; but I wasn't going to admit to something I didn't do.

Finally, he got out of the car, and I went inside the house and called his mother. I told her what happened and asked her if the kids and

I could stay with her that night. She said yes, so I woke the kids up and as I was preparing to leave, he came in the room with the gun in his hand and said, "Lo, it wasn't loaded," as if that was going to change my mind about leaving. It made no difference to me, and I had nothing to say to him as the kids and I went to his mother's house that night.

"Lo, what happened?" she asked when I arrived at her house.

"He saw this stuff in my underwear and he thought I had sex with someone tonight," I said.

"You mean the discharge that is common with women," she said.

"Yeah," I said. "I didn't have sex with anyone and I'm not going back there to live with him; I'm leaving him," I told her.

After that night, I knew I could no longer stay with him. I was not going to ever give him another chance to put a gun to my head, loaded or unloaded. The only person I talked to about that incident was Vincent and I told him I was moving back to Sanford. Because Vincent was still living with his sister and did not have a place of his own, I moved in with my mom. The relationship with Clarence was over. After I moved back to Sanford, Vincent and I spent more time together. All my awake hours, except when I was at work, were spent with him. On most weekends, Vincent got a hotel room and he, I, and the kids went. Clarence still came to my mom's house to see the kids, and he thought I was coming back to him. I had left him before because of the cheating, but I always went back. However, this time it was different. He had never been physically abusive and never ever pulled a gun on me. I did not even know he had a gun. Also, this time was different because I had another relationship interest.

The owner of a restaurant he frequented often said to me, "Big Man says it's not over until he says it's over." He called him "Big Man" because he was a tall guy at six feet six inches.

"Okay, we'll see," I said because I knew it was over between me and him.

Vincent was still selling drugs at that time, but it didn't bother me because we were still just enjoying each other. I was never around him when he sold drugs. Besides, I had a job because I liked making my own money so I would not have to depend on anyone else. After living with my mother for a couple of months, I knew it was time for me to leave there and get my own place. One day while sleeping after work, I was awakened by one of my brothers who was addicted to crack, attempting to take money out of my purse.

"I'm sorry, I wasn't gon take it all," he said when I caught him.

"Yeah, you're sorry alright," I said. I was highly upset by what he was trying to do, and I started sleeping with my purse under my head so I could feel it if he tried to take it again. In another incident, I was preparing for my daughter to begin head start. I purchased school clothes for her and noticed that some of the clothes were missing. Then, I later learned that one of my sisters who was addicted to crack as well had taken the clothes and sold them. However, she played it smart and did not take all the clothes at one time. Instead, she took a dress here and a pair of pants there; so by the time I noticed my daughter's clothes were missing, she had sold most of them. Of course, I told Vincent what was taking place at my mother's house and after talking it over, we decided to get a place together.

We began apartment hunting, and it did not take long for us to agree where we wanted to live. It was a two-bedroom apartment: one bedroom for us and the other for my kids. The kids were excited that we had a place of our own again and so was I. There was no worry about someone coming in while I was asleep and taking my purse to get money for drugs or someone stealing my daughter's clothes to sell them for drugs. Because Vincent sold drugs and did not have a job, I signed the lease and the utilities were in my name, but he paid all the bills.

He also did not have a car of his own yet so while I slept during the day, I allowed him to use my car with the understanding that he would have my car back to me by the time he knew I would be waking up. One day, I woke up and waited for him to bring my car but he did not bring it to me until much later in the day. When he returned home, I asked him where he had been and initially, he lied to me. Later, he told me that he and his friend, the drug dealer, had gone to Miami in my car. "You did what?" I asked in anger because I knew that trip was for drugs. Not only was I upset that he had taken my car to make a drug pickup, but I felt disrespected and believed he disregarded my feelings and the fact that I work hard for my belongings. I had witnessed how the federal drug agents went after innocent family members to get the person they wanted, so him using my car for his drug business did not sit well with me at all. I thought he would have had better judgment but selling drugs had lured him into that life of making fast money and taking indiscriminate risks to make it happen.

One evening, Vincent called me because he heard that the drug agents were sweeping the Sanford area and busting the drug dealers. "Lo, look on the shelf in our closet and get that little sack that my cologne comes in and bring it to me," he said. He wasn't sure if they had been watching him or had received word about what he was doing, so he wanted me to take the drugs out of the apartment to be safe. When I opened the bag, I saw that there were thirteen white round shaped discs inside which I later learned were called cookies. I didn't know he was keeping the drugs in our apartment because we never talked about what he was doing or where. I never saw him selling drugs and I did not want anything to do with it. However, I began to see that I unwillingly and unknowingly did have a lot to do with what he was doing; and I knew that after that incident, things had to change. My thoughts were on my kids knowing that if the drug agents came in that apartment and found those drugs, they could take my kids from me and I could not allow that to happen.

"You can't keep drugs in the apartment like that," I said. "If those people come in here and find drugs, my children could get taken away from me; you have to do something different."

"Lo, I won't bring drugs to our apartment again," he said.

Later, Vincent told me about another incident that happened when he and his friend went to Miami to pick up some drugs. He said that on the ride back, his friend was speeding and they were pulled over by the police. "I kept telling him to slow down, but I guess he was nervous," Vincent said. "Why would you speed if you know you have drugs in the car? Lo, I had the drugs in my lap, and I just knew we were busted. I was so nervous, and I don't know why the cops didn't search us, but I am so glad they didn't." When the police let them go, Vincent said he told his friend not to go over the speed limit the rest of the way home, and he didn't.

After living in Sanford for about six months, we decided to move to Deltona because it was closer to my job, which was in Deland. I was ready to leave Sanford; I wanted to get away from being in the middle of the drama in the projects of the drug boys and the federal drug agents. One day while sitting on my mama's porch, a van drove up and six guys jumped out with guns and started chasing one of the guys from the neighborhood. I learned that the guys in the van were undercover drug agents. The guy from the neighborhood ran around the corner and at the same time he took his shirt off. Then he walked back from around the corner and passed right by the drug agents who were chasing him. The drug agents didn't know who he was because the guy they were chasing was wearing a shirt, so he got away. Another time, the kids were sitting at the edge of the sidewalk playing and two guys came running toward where the kids were sitting shooting at each other.

The gunshots rang out and all I could think about was the kids playing. My sister and I jumped up and ran to grab them to bring them into the house. I had my arms stretched out wide to grab them all, but I think I only grabbed one of them. Again, thankfully, the guys kept running and none of the kids were hurt. Other times, the police patrolled the projects dressed in army fatigue, with big guns, and K-9 dogs on leashes. There was a thick police presence in the projects during that time, especially on the weekends, and I wanted to get away from that scene.

Although we moved to Deltona, Vincent and I still spent a good amount of time in Sanford because he was still selling drugs, and I went to visit my mama and my family regularly. My life was peaceful in Deltona because I went to work, came home, and took care of the kids. I didn't worry about being in or around the drug scene in the projects. Vincent soon purchased a car: it was a 1980 Cadillac Seville, baby blue on the bottom with a white rag top, and he was proud of his car. I, on the other hand, did not like the car because it was the kind of car a dope boy was expected to drive, and I wanted nothing to do with it. I did not want to drive that car nor did I want to ride in it. All the same, I was happy that he had a car because he did not have to use my car to go back and forth to Sanford. He purchased it from a mechanic he trusted, so he knew it was in good condition and it was clean.

Vincent and the guys he sold drugs with used his sister's apartment to do their business. Vincent said he was extra careful about not using the phone at all to talk to anyone he had transactions with about the drugs. But the other guys were not so careful. The police knew that Vincent's friend was a big drug supplier in Sanford, and they were watching him. One evening as Vincent and his friend were returning from the county fair in his friend's car, the police stopped them and dragged them both out of the car. They searched the car in hopes of finding drugs, but all they found was a couple of roaches (the leftover pieces of a marijuana joint), in the ash tray. They arrested them for that and took them to jail.

Vincent said they put him in a separate room from his friend and they questioned him. "When they asked me something, I looked at them like I had no clue what they were talking about. 'Yeah, you are his right-hand man, aren't you?'" he said they asked him. "I didn't say nothing because I knew they didn't have nothing on me. One of them said, 'Look at him, trying to look like he doesn't know anything,' and I just looked at him, Lo, like I didn't know who they were talking about." He stayed in jail overnight and came home the next day.

One evening while we were sitting at home, Vincent got a phone call from one of his drug-dealing associates who lived in Deltona: "Man, they're doing drug busts and they just left my house." Then he received another phone call informing him that they had busted his friend's place as well and that he needed to be careful. Vincent still was not worried about them coming to our house because he believed he had taken the necessary actions to be extra careful, so the police did not know where he lived. "They think I live in Sanford; they don't know I live in Deltona," he assured me.

Later that evening, he went to Sanford, and it was confirmed to him that his friend and some others had been busted by the police and were in jail. What he did not know was that the phone at his sister's apartment and some of the other drug associates' home, had been tapped by the police; and if any names were mentioned during any conversations pertaining to drugs, those people were in danger of being arrested as conspirators to the drug operation. "Lo, that's why I never used the phone at my sister's apartment," he said. Because the others were not careful with phone use, several of them were arrested, went to trial and were convicted and sent to prison for several years. A warrant was issued for one of Vincent's brothers for being a part of that drug operation. One day while he and his brother were riding in his car, the cops pulled them over and arrested his brother on the warrant and arrested Vincent for harboring a fugitive. Because they did not get him in the drug operation sting and because they knew he was a part of it, they tried to get him on a bogus charge of harboring a fugitive when he was only giving his brother a ride. The charge did not hold up and they let him go, but his brother was convicted and sentenced to time in prison.

Chapter 3

Surviving Another Cheat

After the drug busts and the arrests of Vincent's drug friends, I began to talk to him about finding a job because I had had enough. "Baby, you need to find a job and the drug-selling needs to stop," I said. He agreed and not long after that, Vincent got a job working at a company that made embroidery supplies. He seemed to really enjoy working at this new job. That was the first time since living together that I saw him as a working man. He had no problem getting up in the mornings; punctuality was important to him, so he left home with ample time to get to work because he did not want to be late. It was great to have him working on a real job. The pay was not as good as the drug-selling, but I'd rather have him working a legitimate job than an illegal one any day.

Since I worked the graveyard shift at my job, I often went to his place of employment to have lunch with him after getting a couple of hours sleep. One day, I needed to use his car so I had someone take me to his job to get his car. While driving his car, which I did not do often, I lowered the visor, and a piece of folded paper fell out. I opened it and to my surprise, it was a letter from a woman he was seeing. The letter totally blindsided me and I could not believe what I was reading. Finding out that he had been cheating on me was the farthest thing from my mind, but the evidence literally fell in my lap. The woman did not sign the letter so I did not know who she was, but I sure wanted to know. "Is it someone I know?" was one of so many questions that began swirling in my mind. Waiting to pick him up from work that evening seemed like forever because my mind couldn't rest from the unknown of what he had been doing.

I picked him up from work and finally, my questions were answered. I told him about the letter I found and asked, "Have you been seeing someone else?"

"Yes," he said.

"Who is she?" I asked, and he told me her name. I knew her, but I did not really know her.

He went on to say, "Lo, I'm not seeing her anymore, that's why she wrote me that letter; she does not want to stop seeing me." Still, it hurt me to my core that he had been seeing someone else and the deception that goes along with that. I had lived that life before and I did not want to live it again. I knew of one incident he had with another woman while he was selling drugs, but I was hoping that life was over for him. He started cheating with the woman who wrote the letter while he was still selling drugs and it lasted a while. Insisting that it was over, he apologized again and again for it because he saw the hurt it caused me; but his apologies did not make me feel any better.

Here I was again, hurt, disgusted, and feeling the desire to get revenge. However, there is one thing I learned from my experience of having revenge sex when I was with Clarence: I cannot casually have sex with someone without my feelings getting involved. I knew that I loved Vincent, and he loved me. I could've cheated, but I did not want to live in deceit anymore on my part or his. I chose to forgive him, but it took time for the feeling of wanting to cheat to run its course. His actions left me feeling as if I was not enough although he assured me that I was. I had to choose my body many times over my feelings of wanting to hear I was enough from someone else. I did not want to continue the pattern of giving my body to random men. There had to be another way, and I thank God that He gave me that mind.

Eventually, we got past the cheating and to my knowledge, he kept his promise of not cheating again. Although Vincent and I were not married, we started the conversation of having a baby together. I must have been 28 years old at the time. I did not oppose the idea, but I believed my biological clock was ticking. I told him, "I don't want to have children after the age of 30 because I don't want to be raising kids after the age of 50; if you want me to have your baby, we have to start working on it now." I had two kids when we met but he didn't have any kids of his own so I agreed to have a baby with him. After discontinuing birth control and several months of trying, I got pregnant.

Vincent was still working at the embroidery supply company, and we were in a good place in our relationship. However, a couple of months into my pregnancy, the company Vincent worked for closed and he was without a job again. He knew he needed employment, so Vincent started to work for a company that laid cable underground for a little while. Then he worked for a roofing company until he could find something better because he was not satisfied with either of those jobs.

I was still working at my job, and I had good health insurance, but I had to pay a copay each time I went to the doctor during my pregnancy. For one of my appointments, he did not have the money to pay the copay so out of frustration while we were arguing, I yelled, "I hate you!" because I didn't think he was living up to his responsibilities during my pregnancy. My expectations were for him to be there for me when I needed him to be, and he was not. He did not talk to me about his job situation at that time, but I knew it weighed on him and it showed in his countenance. He did not like that he could not help me with my copay when I needed him to. I never asked him if he did, but I believe he dabbled back into selling drugs a little so he could help with the household expenses. In the meantime, he was still looking for a job and a few months before we had our baby, Vincent started working at a welding company that paid well and had great benefits. He was able to give me what I needed when I needed it. Acquiring that job did wonders for his attitude. He began to be more confident and excited about the anticipated arrival of our baby and I began to feel better too.

On January 13, 1991, we welcomed our baby boy and named him Vincent Gerard Paige Jr. After taking a six-week maternity leave from my job, I had to return to work. For the last four weeks, Vincent and I began preparing for him to watch the baby so that when I returned to work, he would be comfortable watching the baby at night. Vincent was all in with the care of the baby. Whenever the baby woke up, Vincent woke up. If it was a bottle the baby needed, he wanted to feed him. Likewise, if the baby needed his diaper changed, he changed it. This was Vincent's first child, and he had never taken care of a newborn baby before, but he was confident that he could do it. I was not as confident, but this is how we decided to do it so we stuck with the plan. The first couple of weeks of Vincent watching the baby went well, so my concerns began to ease up. However, one night after arriving at work and starting my shift, I received a call from Vincent saying, "Lo, I gave him a bottle and he threw all the milk back up."

"What's he doing now?" I asked.

"Nothing, just laying here," he said.

"You want me to come home?" I asked.

"No, I think he's fine, I just wanted to tell you about it," he said.

"Yeah, they do that sometimes," I said. Because I did not hear a sense of urgency in Vincent's voice, I did not get overly worried. "Call me back if you have to, but I think he'll be alright," and he was. I am sure he had never seen that before but I knew that occasionally, the baby will throw up what seems like the entire bottle of milk. I've never seen it be anything serious, so I was pretty sure the baby was fine. That was the one and only time Vincent called me on my job about the baby.

For the four years I had been at my job, the third shift was the only shift I worked; but after having the baby, I thought it would be better for me to switch to the first shift. Getting sufficient sleep on the third shift is difficult enough without having the added responsibility of coming home to care for an infant; so of course, having the baby caused me to have a little more sleep deprivation. I honestly do not know how I did it but as soon as Vincent walked into the house from work, I would hand the baby to him and go to bed. All I needed was three straight hours of sleep then pick up an hour or two here and there, and I could make it. The third shift was so convenient for us because we did not have to worry about a babysitter. If the baby or any of our other kids had to go to the doctor, I was able to take them without either one of us having to take time off from work. However, the lack of sleep started to wear on me after a couple of months, so I began bidding on first shift jobs.

Eventually, I did get a first shift job, working from 7am until 3pm. Vincent and I were both excited because we would be able to not only sleep together at night, but we would be able to spend our evenings together as well. Before the baby, we spent evenings together; but when the baby came, my evenings were devoted mostly to sleep. Along with the shift change, the dilemma of needing a babysitter came as well. I did not know whom I could trust to watch our baby for us while we worked. Because we needed a babysitter quickly, the only person I could think of was my sister Tammy. She was not working at the time and just had a baby three months before I had Vincent Jr. Thankfully, she agreed to watch him until we found a permanent babysitter. I was comfortable with Tammy watching him, but I knew it was too much for her because she had her own small baby to take care of.

Since Vincent worked near Tammy's house, he took the baby there before he went to work and picked him up on the way home. In the meantime, I was inquiring about babysitters in Deland where I worked. One of my coworkers told me about her babysitter who was watching her little girl. She gave me the babysitter's number and I called to ask if she could watch the baby for us and how much she charged. After speaking with her, Vincent and I agreed to have her watch the baby for us. Initially, I was not comfortable with the babysitter because I did not really know her, but the coworker who referred her said she did a very good job with her daughter. As expected, our baby cried the first day I left him with the new babysitter. However, I was not expecting him to still be crying several months later and it left me feeling uncomfortable when I had to leave him. Vincent and I discussed my concerns, and I told him I think it would be better if I went back to the third shift so that he and I could watch the baby again. We knew it was not going to be easy, but we agreed and believed it was best so I went back to the third shift. As far as sleep was concerned, it was more difficult to get sleep because Vincent Jr. was older and much more active. Also, he didn't sleep as much, but with the help of Vincent and our other two kids, who were ten and seven, we did it.

Vincent and I often talked about the pets we had growing up so when Vincent Jr. was a couple of months old, we bought a Chow Chow puppy and named him Bear. He was the cutest little ball of jet-black fur, and he had a low-energy personality. When we brought him home, he hid from us under the beds and only came out to eat and go potty. Also, when he drank water as a puppy, he lazily hung his head over the water bowl and sometimes spent as long as 30 minutes there. I think he did that because of the coolness of the water because as he got older, I noticed his discontent with lying down on the carpet. Whenever he wanted to rest, he went to the kitchen because the tile was cooler.

Vincent Jr. enjoyed playing with Bear and we assumed Bear enjoyed playing with him too. One day as Vincent Jr. was attempting to put a hat on Bear's head, he growled at him. Vincent and I heard him growl but we were not sure if he was growling at the baby. To make sure, Vincent told Vincent Jr. to do it again; so he put the hat on Bear's head and Bear growled again. Instantaneously, Vincent grabbed a stick that we used to put in the track of the sliding glass door and he began to speak to Bear saying, "You see him? Don't you ever growl at him again! You hear me? Don't you ever!" He whacked him across his back about three times with that stick. Bear yelped in pain each time he hit him.

"Vincent, you gon kill him," I said.

"If he ever growl at Poogy (that is what we call Vincent Jr.) again, I will kill him!" Vincent said. I thought the punishment he gave Bear was harsh and I did not think Bear understood Vincent. However, Vincent Jr. played with Bear after that incident, put the hat on his head and did other things but Bear never growled at him again. There was another incident when Vincent was feeding Bear, and he reached to grab Bear's bowl and Bear growled at him. He hit Bear on the side of his mouth with his fist and said, "Who you growling at, huh? Don't you ever growl at me; I feed you!" Bear never growled at him again. Other than those two times, I never saw Vincent discipline Bear in that way because after establishing who was in charge, he did not have to.

Despite the way he chose to let Bear know who was in charge, Vincent loved that dog and Bear loved him. When he came home from work, Bear would walk up to him wagging his tail and Vincent would get down on his knees. He and Bear would push each other like they were two dogs playing. Bear put his teeth on Vincent's arms but never bit down on him, and this playing would last for ten minutes or more. Vincent talked to him saying, "Hey Bear, hey boy," in a playful voice while rubbing him down and Bear would make a barking howling noise as if he was trying to talk back to him.

Bear was also very protective of us. Vincent and I were sitting outside with him one day when the mailman came. He walked up to Bear as if he was going to pet him, but Bear started growling and the mailman stopped. "He usually lets me pet him; he's never done this before," the mailman said. Sometimes we would put Bear outside on his leash and apparently when the mailman came up to deliver the mail, Bear allowed him to pet him. "He's usually very friendly; I don't know why he's reacting this way. It must be because you all are out here with him," the mailman said. It was not vicious growl, but Bear growled just enough to let the mailman know that now is not a good time to pet me and the mailman understood.

There was another instance that Vincent's cousins came over to the house and we were all sitting in the living room, and Vincent was sitting in the chair with Vincent Jr. in his lap. Bear lay down next to the chair Vincent sat in. Then one of Vincent's cousins stood up to hold the baby and Bear stood up and growled. The cousin sat back down in his chair and Vincent let Bear know it was all right. "You stood up too fast man," Vincent told his cousin. Bear was not vicious, and he never bit anyone, but he did not hesitate to act if he thought our safety was in danger.

Bear was with us for thirteen years before we had him put down. We began noticing the difficulty he was having getting up and sitting down. It progressively worsened over a couple of years, so we made the tough decision to have him put down. Vincent made the appointment with the veterinarian for a Saturday so he would be able to take him. We informed the children of our decision and they had their time to say goodbye to Bear before that day came. We woke up early that Saturday morning to take Bear to the vet and I thought I would be able to go with them; but when the time came, I said, "I can't go."

"Okay," Vincent said because he understood why, so he and Bear went alone. I waited for him to come home and when he did, his eyes were still red from crying. "I held him in my arms until he stopped breathing. Lo, I tried to hold back the tears, but I couldn't."

"See, that's why I couldn't go," I said. "I know I would've been a bag of water." Bear was a great family pet and after we put him down, we agreed that we were not getting any more dogs because we knew there would never be another Bear.

Chapter 4

The Next Step

Unfortunately, the welding company Vincent worked at closed so he was without a job again. He went back to the roofing company he was at before and worked there while continuing to pursue a better job. A few months later, he walked into Invacare Corporation to fill out an application. The human resources department told him that they usually did not take applications from walk-ins, but they made an exception for him. Usually, the applicant had to apply through a temporary staffing agency and if Invacare wanted to hire the applicant permanently after several months, they would. "Lo, the Lord gave me that job," Vincent said because Invacare hired him and he didn't have to go through the temporary staffing agency. Initially, he started working on the assembly line, but he did not stay at that position long. "I am bidding on another position as soon as I'm able to. Lo, I can't stay on that assembly line." When he was at the job long enough to bid on open positions, he was soon off the assembly line. Vincent held various positions at Invacare until he got a position in shipping and receiving as the lead person. "The Lord created that position for me because that wasn't even a position at Invacare." Vincent was so thankful for his job and he was well liked and respected by his coworkers.

In 1994, Vincent and I started discussing marriage. At that time, we had been together for about six years and had three kids (the two I had when we met and the one we had together) so it was obvious to us that marriage should be our next step. Ideally, marriage should have come before we had a child together but our thinking was backwards at the time. Also, we started the process of purchasing a home that year. The housing market was good for buyers, so I took a class for first-time home buyers and was presented with a certificate to receive down payment and closing costs assistance. After acquiring a realtor to assist with the home search, we agreed upon a home in Deltona which is where we were residing at the time. The home was in foreclosure and needed some renovations before we moved in. With the help of the realtor, we were able to purchase the home for what we thought was a very reasonable price even with the renovations included. We were told the renovations were going to take approximately three weeks. Since we had moved out of our rental, my sister Tammy allowed us to live with her. At the end of the three weeks, our home was ready and in June of 1994, we moved into a four-bedroom, two-bath home and the mortgage payment was less than what we had been paying in rent. We were thrilled!

After we purchased a home, we talked about marriage a little more seriously. I was ready to get married because we were a family with a newly purchased home. Vincent was hesitant about the whole marriage and commitment thing because he said forever was a long time and he didn't know if he could commit to it. "We have invested six years into this relationship and ain't neither one of us going nowhere," I said.

"Yeah, but I don't know if I'm ready for that commitment," Vincent said. The subject of marriage would come up in conversation here and there but that's all it was, just talk. I didn't want to have invested all that time in a relationship and not have anything to show for it. He called me his lady and I was, but I wanted to take the next step and be his wife.

In August of that same year, we got an early morning phone call at about 2:30am. I didn't answer because I had a dear family member who had a habit of calling in the wee hours of the night while drunk and still drinking and I didn't feel like talking that night, so I let the phone ring until it stopped. Then the phone began to ring again and I hesitantly answered because I thought it might have been an emergency. "Hello," I said.

"Hello," the voice on the phone said, "Loretta, Eldred has been shot six times and he has been airlifted to ORMC and it does not look good for him." It was my oldest sister Linda calling to inform me that one of our brothers had been shot.

"What?" I asked in disbelief, making sure I heard her correctly.

"Eldred's been shot," she said again.

"Six times?" I asked.

"Yes," she said.

"Okay, I'm going to the hospital," I said.

"Come by and pick me up," she said.

"Okay," I said.

I hung up the phone and said to Vincent, "Eldred's been shot six times and he has been airlifted to ORMC. We have to go." Without hesitation, we both got dressed and headed to the hospital, picking up my sister Linda from her house to ride with us. I thought to myself, "Six times? He's not gonna make it." "Do they know who shot him and why?" I asked Linda. I couldn't understand why someone would want to shoot Eldred because he was silly and always clowning, but he did not bother anyone. Linda only knew what she had told me, so she did not have the answers to my questions.

When we arrived at the hospital, Eldred was in surgery and several family members were sitting in the waiting room, including my mom and my oldest brother Tony. Eldred lived in his own apartment across from my cousin's girlfriend so when she heard the gunshots and saw that it was Eldred, she called my cousin who in turn called my brother Tony. She said when she looked outside, she saw Eldred crawling on the ground. "When I got there, I saw Eldred fighting for his life and that was all I needed to see," Tony said. He went on to say definitively, "He gon make it." Everyone else was upset, but he was calmly putting cream and sugar in his coffee telling all of us, "He's alright, he's gon make it." The image of the peaceful calm Tony had and the faith that Eldred was going to make it never left me. Anytime I wanted to get upset, I thought about his peace and his faith.

After the surgery, the doctor came in to inform us of his condition. "He was shot six times, one in the carotid artery in his neck and we had to give him eight pints of blood. We were able to remove four of the bullets, but we left two in him because they will not cause any harm. The chances of him surviving this is not good." The doctor went on to say, "You all can't see him right now, but you can see him later today." Vincent and I went home and returned to the hospital later in the evening. When we went in to see Eldred, he appeared as if he was seizing because his whole body continuously tremored. Everyone was allowed to go in and see him, including his friends. I was uneasy with friends going in because we did not know who had shot him. We later learned that the bullets came from two guns so there were two shooters.

"Elk, man, you can't die; I'm gonna marry your sister and you have to be there," Vincent said. I was surprised and pleased to hear him say that because we had only discussed marriage but there were no final plans. Furthermore, we had not discussed it often so to hear him say that to Eldred let me know that it was on his mind. After two months of being in the hospital and spending a month in rehab, Vincent and I brought Eldred to our house where he continued his rehab. The bullet to the carotid artery on the right side caused a stroke-like condition on his left side and his sight was damaged as well. He had 20/20 vision, but now the signal takes an extra second or two to go from the object he looks at to his brain, so he must give his brain that extra time to see what he is looking at. Eldred lived with us for about two months and progressed. Then he went to live with our mom where he progressed even more, and later he went on to get his own apartment where he still resides today.

We later learned that my youngest brother Eric was also in the apartment at the time of the shooting, but he was not hurt. The story is that they heard a loud knock at the door and someone yelling, "Elk, open this door!" Then Eric said he heard the gunshots. When Eldred was well enough to speak, he said he thought it was one of our nephews knocking at the door but when he went to open the door, they started shooting. "All I remember is spinning in circles as the bullets were hitting me." Eventually, there was an arrest and conviction in the shooting of Eldred.

On February 14, 1995 (Valentine's Day), Vincent and I were sitting on the riverfront talking and relaxing after coming from dinner. While we were talking, he got out of the car, came around to the passenger side, opened my door, got on one knee with a ring in hand, and asked me to be his wife. I do not remember his exact words, so I cannot quote him. However, I do remember him asking, "Will you marry me?" And of course, I said yes. Vincent surprised me when he proposed in such a formal way because as far as our relationship was concerned, all the formalities were out the window. Vincent and I had been living together for six years and we had a child together. That is one of those 'let's just go the courthouse' situations. However, that was not the way it was for him, and he relished making momentous occasions special. He told my sister Gail that he was going to ask me to marry him before he proposed. Usually, the groom to be asks the parents of the bride to be for her hand in marriage. Vincent knew I would have married him without the approval of anyone in my family, but he asked Gail because he wanted approval from someone about his plans and she gave it to him.

Immediately, Vincent and I set out to choose a date for our wedding. We chose April 1st, oblivious to the fact that it was April Fool's Day. Someone had to bring that to our attention, which did not change our minds or alter our wedding date. We wanted a minister to marry us, but neither one of us was a member of a church. We asked my brother Tony to ask his pastor if he would marry us. Since I knew his pastor and his wife, I wanted him to officiate our ceremony but his requirement for us to take six months of marriage counseling first would have taken too long, so we had to find someone else to marry us. We understood his decision, but I was disappointed that he was not doing the ceremony. The search was on to find another minister to marry us, so I asked my cousin Debra to ask her pastor to do our ceremony. Thankfully, he agreed to do it.

Because Vincent and I had lived together for several years, we just wanted to be married and did not feel the need for a big extravagant wedding. I just wanted a small wedding with family and friends in attendance. My friend Geralyn was my maid of honor and Victor was Vincent's best man. At that time, I didn't have a close relationship with my father, so my brother Tony walked me down the aisle and the rest of the wedding party included our children and nieces. Delrick was Vincent's groomsman and Fantasy was my bridesmaid. Vincent Jr. was our ringbearer and our nieces Jafaye and Shakira were the flower girls. We wanted an outside wedding since we were not members of a church so the venue we chose for our wedding was The Gazebo which sat in the center of a manicured lawn in Sanford. We had our wedding reception conveniently across the street from The Gazebo so after the ceremony, our guests had a short walk to the reception hall. The colors for our wedding were burgundy and beige and although I was not a virgin, my wedding dress was white. My sister, Linda (who is the decorator and crafts person in our family) made my wedding veil and all the flowers, including my bouquet. She did all the decorating at The Gazebo and the wedding reception venue.

At the time, Victor was living in The Bronx, and my sister, Jonita, was living in Long Island, so, they decided to ride down together from New York for our wedding along with their significant others. They arrived two days before our wedding and it was "on like popcorn" because Victor was in town. Vincent had a happy smile that was unmatched and on full display. Also, Vincent's childhood friend Bernard came from Rochester, New York. Our family had the preparations in full effect for our big day. My brother Mike saw Vincent and I riding in town, waved us down to stop, gave us money and said, "Y'all use this to help with your wedding," and my brother Dwight rented a limo to take me to the wedding.

When people ask me about our wedding, I tell them we had a ghetto wedding because we did not have a wedding coordinator or a professional photographer like most people. We just winged it, but it was still amazing! We did not even think about a wedding rehearsal, which was totally okay, because it stormed the evening before; and since our wedding was outside, we would not have been able to rehearse at our outside venue. Vincent and I went along with the tradition of not seeing each other before the wedding, so he and all the guys stayed at his uncle Joe's house the night before, and the girls stayed at our house with me.

On the morning of our wedding day, it was still raining and cloudy outside; but because we were finishing the preparations, we did not have time to dwell on the weather. The girls and I dressed at Linda's house. Our wedding time was 3:30 in the afternoon, but me and the girls arrived an hour late. I was ready but one of my flower girls arrived at Linda's house late and because I wanted all the girls in my wedding party to ride in the limo with me, we did not leave until everyone was there. Of course, Vincent and his guys were on time because Vincent was a stickler about that. I think if he were in my shoes, we would have had only one flower girl in our wedding because he would not have waited that long (maybe a few minutes, but not an hour).

We finally arrived at The Gazebo and our family and friends were waiting. As the limousine was coming up to the venue, I saw Vincent and Victor walking back toward The Gazebo and letting others know we were finally there. By this time, the rain had stopped but the skies were still overcast; the sun peeked through every now and then. The weather wasn't ideal, but seeing the faces of family and friends was enough sunshine for us. Linda gave the instructions to the wedding party as to how and when to walk up the steps and down the aisle to the front of The Gazebo. The ladies and I stayed in the limousine until Linda instructed each of us to come out. Vincent and Victor walked up together, then Delrick, Geralyn, and Fantasy each walked up alone in that order. After that Vincent Jr. walked up as the ring bearer. My brother Dwight and my brother-in-law Rodney unrolled the runner for me to walk down the aisle after the flower girls walked down.

Finally, it was my turn to step out of the limousine. "Ooooh," gasped several of the guests as I exited the limousine. My brother Tony stood waiting for me. Linda gave me my last onceover before we walked down the aisle. Tony grabbed my hand and we embraced our fingers together while all eyes were on us. I do not know who was more nervous, me or him; but being the jokester he was, he said something funny, and we both laughed before walking up the stairs as "For Your Love" by Stevie Wonder began to play. Then as "Here Comes the Bride" began to play, he wrapped my arm in his and we walked down the aisle. Despite the weather, it made my heart smile to see our family and friends who still came to support us on our wedding day. Our mothers were there and my brothers and sisters, including Eldred, as well as Vincent's brothers and sisters. Also, Joe and Horace, beloved uncles on Vincent's side of the family were there and in full participation. Uncle Horace and Vincent's sister Denise were our videographers that we didn't know about until the wedding started, which is another thing we didn't think about but our family had our backs. Our wedding was not professionally coordinated and planned, but it was a beautiful display of familial love and support.

As Vincent and I stood before the minister, the skies were still overcast but the dark clouds could not suppress the brightness of the sun as it shined down on us like a spotlight from heaven. We both noticed it because I later asked Vincent, "Did you see the sun shining through the clouds?"

"Yeah, and I believe that was a sign that the Lord put His blessing on our marriage," he said. I did not think of it that deeply, but I know I will never forget it. After we said our vows and had our first kiss as husband and wife, our cousin Tameka sang "Endless Love" by Luther Vandross and Mariah Carey as we lit the unity candle. We had given her a tape with the instrumentals of the song so she could rehearse and be ready for our wedding but she did not bring the tape with her to the wedding. Therefore, she sang the song acapella, and if our guests had not seen the confusion of finding out she did not have the tape, they would have thought that was the plan because she did an amazing job without the music.

After taking pictures with our on-the-spot, photographer who was at the wedding with Vincent's brother, whose name is also Tony, the wedding party entered the limousine and other guests followed in their cars as we rode through our neighborhood blowing the car horns. Upon returning to the reception venue, some guests were standing outside and some were seated inside. Before we went inside, all the guests had to go inside and Linda announced the wedding party as we entered the building and took our seats at our table. Although we did dance, I do not remember us having a first dance. We did all the other traditions such as toasts to bride and groom after dinner by the best man and the maid of honor, throwing the bouquet, throwing the garter, and cutting the cake.

At the reception, I consumed a little alcohol because my plans were to let go and enjoy my wedding night. I had bought a sexy red negligee to put on for my husband and I was ready. We had everything packed for our wedding night. We left the reception and went to the hotel after stopping to get something to eat because the food we ate at our wedding reception was long gone and we were hungry. I guess dancing and talking to family and friends made us work up an appetite. Then we arrived at the hotel and we went to our room. Still feeling a little tipsy, I went to the bathroom to change as Vincent lay in bed and waited for me to come out. I freshened up a bit and attempted to put on my negligee without making too much noise. "You alright in there?" Vincent asked while I was in the bathroom.

"Yeah," I said laughing because I could not keep my balance while I slipped into the negligee and I fell back against the wall a couple of times. It was hilarious to me because I knew I was a little tipsy. I walked out of the bathroom and Vincent sat up in bed with a big grin on his face, so I assumed he liked what he saw. But it was not long before that negligee was off and we made good love for the first time as husband and wife. Both of us must have been tired because after one round of lovemaking, we woke up hours later with me on top of him. I do not usually drool when I sleep, but I had to wipe my mouth and his chest. "That didn't go as planned," I said as we laughed while I rolled off him and we both snuggled under the covers and went back to sleep.

Chapter 5

Against All Odds

If the success of our marriage was contingent on what we saw displayed before us in the homes we grew up in, then we were doomed to fail because neither one of us grew up in homes with successful, healthy marriages. Vincent's mother and father were married, but their marital relationship was toxic because Vincent's father was an alcoholic and extremely abusive to his mother, both physically and mentally. Also, he was physically abusive to Vincent and his siblings. Vincent told me about an incident in which his father hit his mother in the eye with the back end of a hammer and it caused her to lose sight in that eye. He also told me of another incident in which his father had another woman living in the house with them and he punched the other woman in the mouth: "Lo, now this was crazy, because he hurt the hand he punched her with. My mom stood bandaging the hand he hurt, while my father sat across the table from the other woman; he held a gun in the other hand and told her, if she moves, he will kill her."

Vincent told me of the time his older sister took his younger sister with her to steal from a department store. They were detained by security. Security contacted his father and he went and picked them up from the store. After he returned home from picking them up from the store, he whipped them and he accidentally hit his youngest sibling bruising him badly. Child Protective Services got involved when they saw the bruise on him. After they investigated, they gave Vincent's mom an ultimatum and said that either his father had to leave the home or they were taking the children. Out of fear of their father, his mom chose their father to stay in the home which did not please Vincent and his other siblings. Child Protective Services took the three youngest children and placed them in the foster care system where they remained until they were almost grown.

When Vincent spoke about the incident of Child Protective Services taking his three younger siblings away, he said, "Lo, it was so sad because it was right before Christmas. They used to run away from the foster family to come back home, so Child Protective Services moved them further away from us. One morning we woke up and we saw their footprints in the snow, so we knew they had tried to come home but we didn't see them." Vincent's mom endured years of abuse from his father and during those years, she left him several times but she kept going back to him. It wasn't until years later, after all the kids were grown and on their own that she finally left him for good.

My mom was married to my father, but he left when I was seven years old. He was also an alcoholic and abusive to my mother. There were numerous times that I saw my father walk in the house and without saying a word, he would lunge at my mama and they would both fall to the floor fighting. One time, he walked into the house and started fighting my mama and my oldest sister Linda yelled at him. "Uhn uhn n***a not here!" She hit him with a glass cup that she was holding in her hand, shattering the cup. "If you gon beat her, you betta do it out there and not here!"

In another instance he came home and jumped on my mama and Linda grabbed an empty milk container, which was glass in those days. She threw it in his back while he was on top of my mama on the floor and the glass shattered everywhere. Linda helped my mama each time without even thinking about it while the rest of us just watched. My mom laughs as she tells of the time Linda grabbed a bat to hit my father with: "I looked up and Linda had the bat ready to swing it. No, Linda!" she yelled while waving her hand, but the bat was already in motion coming down and it landed on my mom's knee. After the fights, they must've made up because it seemed like all was well or maybe I was just too young to understand.

My father worked in construction and each day when he returned home from work, me and some of my other siblings ran out to meet him. We'd take his lunch pail and anything else he was carrying because we were glad daddy was home. One day, we waited at the window like we normally did around the time he was to arrive home from work. We waited and waited, but he did not come home. "Mama where is Daddy?" we asked.

"I don't know," was her response but thinking back, she did not seem bothered that he did not come home. At seven years old, I did not understand relationships and marital problems, so I expected him to always come home. The next day, we did the same thing: we sat at the window and waited for him to come home but he didn't. I do not know how many days we sat at that window peering out, hoping, and waiting for him to come home, but he never did. Eventually, we stopped going to the window to wait for him to come home because it was evident that it was not going to happen.

Even though he sometimes came home raising hell, he was my daddy and I loved him. Some months later, he returned home for a few minutes to see us but I was not there. "Lo, daddy came home," I heard my brothers and sisters excitedly saying when I returned home. I was upset that I missed my daddy when he came to visit us, and I was hoping he would come back but he didn't. I still remember feeling the regret of not being home when he came by because I really wanted to see him. The next time I saw him was over 20 years later and after I found him, I made it a priority to visit him at least once every year until his death. My mom never said a harsh word about my daddy and she never remarried. They didn't get a divorce but remained separated until his death. She had male friends who would come over sometimes and a few stayed a night or two here and there, but there was never another male figure in my life who I called 'daddy.' My mom went on to have more kids after my daddy left, but the fathers of those kids never took care of them; she was on her own, a single mother of twelve children.

Vincent and I did not think about our parents or their marriages before we were married because we did not realize how much of an influence the households we grew up in had shaped our lives and our way of thinking. Vincent was never physically abusive; however, we did have a couple of physical altercations before we were married, but he never hit me. I wish I could say the same for me, but I cannot. There were a few times I tried to fight him. I do remember one time when he held me to restrain me and in doing so, he cupped my face tightly with his hand and his fingernails left marks on my face.

After we were married, we had an argument in which he got physical but not with me. I was lying in bed one evening resting before I had to go to work. Vincent came home intoxicated and wanted to argue. Because I was not engaged at all, it angered him even more. He was obviously upset, but I would rather he talked to me when he was sober. He tried and tried to argue with me, but I would not even look at him. Finally, he walked away and he kicked a mirror that was standing in our bedroom trying to break it, but it did not break. "Ugh," he said when he kicked the mirror, and I chuckled because that mirror was more difficult to break than he thought. A couple of days later, we talked and laughed about what happened and how he was so upset that I would not argue with him. "Better me kicking the mirror than kicking you," he said.

"You got that right," I said, as we both laughed.

In the years before we were married when Vincent was selling drugs, he paid all the bills; but when he started working, we split the household bills down the middle. When he got his paycheck, he asked me how much he needed to contribute for the bills. I told him, and he gave me the money; that worked for us. However, soon after we got married, that changed for me. He came in as usual and asked, "Lo, how much are the bills this week?"

"No, Vincent, we can't do it like that no more. We're married now and our money should be put together." That was the way I thought it should be when we got married. I did not think there should be any more of my money or your money, but our money. Vincent knew I was not one to spend money frivolously, so he had no problem with us putting our money together. Since I already had a bank account, I added his name to my account and that is how we began our marriage. There was no more yours and mine, it was now ours. Vincent kept a few dollars out of his paycheck to put in his pocket, but most of it went into our account. God started working in our marriage by giving us wisdom to become one in our finances even though we had not yet committed our lives to Him.

After about a year of being married, God began to draw us to Him. That was the beginning of having the odds stacked in our favor for a healthy successful marriage. Vincent and I started visiting the church my brother Tony attended. I grew up going to church, but I wasn't totally committed to it. Conversely, Vincent did not have any church involvement. One day while we were riding in the car talking, I asked, "Vincent, why ain't you in jail? Why didn't you go to jail with the rest of 'em?" I was referring to those who had gone to prison after all the drug busts that happened years before. "It's only by the grace of God that you didn't go to prison too," I said and he agreed. God brought all that to my mind. I did not know what was happening, but the Lord was drawing both of us to Him.

"Lo, on the night before our wedding, me, Victor, and the boys were getting high and I told them there's one more thing I have to do and that is give my life to the Lord. 'Aw, man, don't nobody wanna talk about that now,'" was their response because we were in the middle of getting high, so they did not want to mess up their high by talking about the Lord. "I didn't talk about it anymore that night but I knew I had to do it though."

I began having dreams about God and I knew this girl on my job who always talked about the Lord, so I told her about my dreams. "See you special. He's drawing you; He wants you," she said. I did not know what that meant at the time, but I listened to her and I later learned it was the goodness of God drawing us to Him.

After visiting my brother's church a few times, Vincent wanted to join the church but I was not feeling the same way. I knew where the pastor and most members of that church had come from spiritually and I did not know if I wanted to be a part of it. I used to attend the church that they had come from, and it was heavily legislated by man's traditions such as women could not wear jewelry, pants or makeup. I just did not want to be a part of that. Also, I thought the pastor from the church that most of them come out of was gay and that most of the guys who went to the church were gay as well. When I visited my brother's church and heard the pastor say, 'Baby, let me tell you,' while he was preaching, I thought, "Oh, yeah, he must be gay too." What man says that while he is speaking to both women and men? "Vincent, let's go visit my friend's church who lives in DeLand", I suggested.

Vincent did not have a problem with the pastor saying 'baby' in addressing the congregation while he preached. He said, "Lo, you can go where you wanna go, but I'm going to Calvary," which was my brother's church. He started going every Sunday and I reluctantly visited sometimes. If I did not go with him, he would take Vincent Jr.

I worked some Saturday nights while still on the third shift at my job. During the ride home on Sunday mornings, I would hear gospel songs playing on the radio. Sometimes when I got home, I would be crying while listening to the music, run into the house, turn the radio on and say, "Vincent, listen to this." We both would start singing and praising God. We knew something was happening to us, but I did not want to fully give in to it. I did not want to become a member at my brother's church, but Vincent was ready to join. I did not want what I had experienced with church before, I just wanted God. Eventually, the desire for God overtook any reservations I had about the pastor, the church, and my past experiences.

I knew we had to be in a church that taught we needed to be born again, be baptized and receive the gift of the Holy Spirit for salvation; that is what they taught at Calvary. I had been baptized, but I had never received the Holy Spirit; I believed the gift was real and I wanted it.

One Sunday morning as Vincent and I sat in service, the pastor was preaching about the flood in the days of Noah and the one comment that resonated with me was when he said, "I can imagine as the flood waters rose, the parents were holding their kids over their heads, trying to save them from drowning in the rising waters." All I could think about was our son Delrick because the previous day, he was caught stealing at a store.

I was lying in bed asleep from working the night before when the phone rang. Answering the phone, I said, "Hello?"

"Hello, Mrs. Paige?" the caller said.

"Yes," I answered.

"We need you to come down to the store because we have your son here for attempting to steal a hair pick." the caller continued.

"You caught him trying to steal a hair pic?" I asked.

"Yes, and the only reason we did not call the police is because he answered us 'No sir' and 'Yes sir,' so we knew he had good parents."

"Thank you, sir, we are on our way," I responded. Hanging the phone up I yelled, "Vincent, D got caught stealing out of the store and we have to go get him." I hurriedly got dressed and we headed to the store wondering why he was trying to steal. To add to the ridiculousness, the man who called me said our son had enough money in his pocket to pay for the pick. When we arrived at the store, we let the employee know who we were and she took us to a room in the back. There our son was sitting in a chair and crying because he knew he was in trouble. After talking to the managers, we thanked them again for not calling the police. We took our son home and both of us whipped his behind. So when the pastor preached that he could imagine the parents holding their kids over their heads to save them as the flood waters rose, all I could think about was saving our son. I believed that surrendering my life to God was a step in the right direction.

At the end of his sermon, the pastor gave an altar call for anyone who wanted to be saved so I went. As I got up to go to the altar, Vincent got up as well and we both went. One of the ladies from the church came up and started praying with me. With tears flowing, I began to weep because I wanted God. I did not know what to pray, but the lady praying with me helped by encouraging me as I cried out to the Lord while one of the men was praying with Vincent. After we finished praying at the altar, the pastor said they were having special prayer the following Friday night for all those who wanted to receive the baptism of the Holy Spirit and we knew we needed that.

Me, Vincent, my sister Gail, and others came that Friday night to receive the Holy Spirit and I was ready. After getting instructions, we kneeled and began praying. All who wanted to receive the Holy Spirit had someone praying with them and they told us when we receive the Holy Spirit, we will begin to speak with other tongues. I had heard people do it before, but I had never spoken with other tongues and was not sure if I would. I wanted God and if that included speaking with other tongues, then I wanted it. One of the older ladies from the church prayed with me. She was from Jamaica and with her Jamaican accent she said, "Say thank you, Jesus," and I did.

"Thank you, Jesus. Lord I want you!" I began to say as I cried out to God. I also remembered talking to another girl from my job who had received the Holy Spirit and she told me to praise God by saying, 'Hallelujah, Lord I praise you!' so I said that too. After doing that for about five minutes, I started speaking in other tongues. It was happening to me; I heard myself. God had taken control of my tongue and I did not know what I was saying, but I knew it was the Holy Spirit. At that moment, I felt like me and God were the only ones in the church; I spoke in other tongues for a while. Then at the end of the service, those who were praying with us told me that my sister Gail and one other lady had also received the Holy Spirit. Vincent did not receive it that night, but we were back at church for prayer on the following Tuesday night and Vincent received the Holy Spirit and began to speak in other tongues. He was baptized the following Sunday. When we tell others how God was drawing both of us to Him at the same time, some did not believe us. 'Did you get saved because she got saved?' or vice versa was a question we were often asked. Neither one of us got saved because the other one did, so we knew it was God's doing.

All of this happened about two weeks before we celebrated our one-year wedding anniversary. So here we were, babes in our marriage and in the Lord; but we were all in and hungry for more. The church had service on Sunday morning, Sunday evening, Tuesday evening, and Wednesday evening and we were at them all. We were also in the new member classes on Tuesday evenings before the prayer service. I know it seems like a lot of church, but it did not seem that way to us. We were excited about what we were learning about the Lord as well as the relationships we were building with the members of the church. After completing the new member classes, we joined the choir and Vincent became an usher. Because of our faithfulness and promptness to service, the pastor gave Vincent a key to open and close the church for the services. Later we became assistants with the youth department and ordained as deacons in addition to the ministries we were already involved in. So now we were also at the church on Saturday afternoons for youth service and we were enthralled with all of it.

Chapter 6

God's Marriage Classes

Vincent and I were enjoying our married life and newfound life in Christ and as far as I was concerned, I thought we had a good marriage. We had lived together for seven years, so we knew what we were getting in each other. He was a good husband to me and I was a good wife to him. We had purchased our home and a new van. The kids were not too happy about having to attend church so often, but they went with it because they had no choice. Overall, we were happy with our lives. Although we had what we considered a good marriage, we did not have a God marriage so He began to tear down what we were building so that He could build it the way He wanted it.

As soon as we joined the church, we started paying tithes and offerings although we were advised by our pastor not to do so until we were taught and had understanding as to why it should be done. "Oh, no, we want to start now," was our response to our pastor and we did. We were not having any financial problems and we wanted to please God, so there was no hesitation. Then after a while, I noticed our finances began to get constricted and we fell behind in our payments on the van; but we still paid our tithes and offerings. That was the first time I was unsure of what to do with our finances. I was usually on top of the finances, making sure that the bills were paid on time because I wanted my credit to remain in good standing. I had two bank accounts, one with my credit union at my job and the one Vincent and I shared. Having good credit and managing our finances were high on my priority list. I was told by an older woman I often talked to on my job that good credit was as good as gold because it gives you purchasing power. The things I considered valuable and had learned to depend on such as my finances and good credit were in jeopardy. Vincent did not have good credit when we got married because he was delinquent in repaying student loans that he had taken out to go to college, so the house and the van were in my name.

In the meantime, we had purchased an older model Honda two-door hatchback with a manual transmission as our second car that we paid for with cash. I did not know how to drive a stick shift, so Vincent took me out driving to teach me. While driving the car, I was already nervous and Vincent made me more nervous with his instructions. Of course, the car stalled several times while I was driving because I could not get that balance between easing off the clutch and pressing the gas. "My goodness, Lo, just press the gas when you take your foot off the clutch to go," he said. He had a way of saying "My goodness" that when he said it, his frustration and impatience could be heard as if he was saying, "It's so simple, why are you making it so hard?" That frustrated me.

After a few minutes of him being my driving instructor, I felt it was hopeless trying to learn to drive the car with him in it, so I immediately stopped the car and said, "You get this car," as I opened the door and went around to get in the passenger seat. "I can't learn to drive this car with you," I said. The following day, I took the keys and drove the car by myself. I was determined to learn how to drive the car. I was fine until I came to a stop sign on a hill and could not maneuver the clutch and gas to go up that hill. Beckoning for the cars to go around me with my hand, I waited until there was no one behind me. Then I floored that gas as I took my foot off the clutch to get up the hill. When I returned home, I told Vincent what happened on the hill and we both laughed about it. After that, I continued to take the car out until I mastered the manual transmission shifting.

During that time, I did not know if it was Vincent or God who was rubbing me the wrong way; I say the 'wrong way' because I did not like the feeling. In my desire to please God, I wanted to be the wife I needed to be to Vincent, but I felt like I was losing myself and it did not feel good. Before I had a desire to please God, my life was mostly about pleasing me and being the wife I needed to be to Vincent was not a priority. I had to make sure Loretta was taken care of and Vincent got what was left. I was trying to hold on to who I was and please God, but God was not having that. Instead of blaming God for my frustrations, I blamed Vincent. Vincent never had a problem informing me or others as to his feelings. If he had a problem with you or something you did, he would let you know but I held my feelings in. If I thought sharing my feelings would cause confrontation, then they were better left unsaid and my frustration manifested in my attitude. It was nothing for me to go a week without talking to my husband because I did not know how to share my feelings. I did not care about not talking to him because he frustrated me. But when it became my desire to please God, He made it uncomfortable for me to keep that attitude.

One morning, I went to my place for my prayer time with God as I did each day and Vincent had already left for work. I was not talking to him, so I did not say anything to him before he left. When I went for my prayer time, I was interrupted by a thought that came to me so strong to call Vincent and ask him to forgive me. "Forgive me for what?" I thought. "What did I do?" Again, the thought came to me, "Call Vincent and ask him to forgive you," and I knew it was the Lord. This is one of those times that God was rubbing me the wrong way because I did not understand why I had to ask Vincent for forgiveness when he had done something that irritated me. Nevertheless, wanting to please God, I called him on his job and said, "Vincent forgive me; I was wrong," expecting him to say the same thing to me. Instead, he went in even more telling me what I did wrong. I had to take it and said, "You're right, babe, and I'm sorry."

Later, I realized that I was wrong because I should not have expected him to know how I felt if I did not tell him. "Lo, I am not a mind reader; if you don't tell me, how can I know?" he asked.

"You're right, bae," I said. Asking for forgiveness meant admitting that I was wrong, which was not an easy thing for me to do but I realized that it took nothing from me to ask for forgiveness.

While riding in the car on a Sunday morning headed to church, the Lord checked me again. Vincent did something that really annoyed me, and I thought to myself, "Ugh, he's really getting on my nerves." What he did exactly, I can't recall but I remember the incident because it was eye-opening for me.

As I thought how annoyed I was at what Vincent did, the Lord checked me and asked, "Didn't you just do that?"

"Yes, I did just do that," I thought. I had just done the same thing and if the Lord had not shown me that, I probably would not have noticed it. It was easy for me to see how Vincent annoyed me, but I didn't notice when I had done the same thing. If I had just done the same thing, then he must have been annoyed with me as well.

I immediately told him what happened: "Vincent, I was just thinking how much you get on my nerves when you did that, and the Lord showed me that I just did the same thing. I guess just like you get on my nerves, I get on your nerves too," I said.

"Yes, you do," he said emphatically, and we laughed about it. It wasn't important for me to remember what he did that got on my nerves. Remembering that I got on his nerves too was the important part. I was so quick to look at him as being the problem but not to look at myself. That day, the Lord showed me myself and it changed my perception of me. I learned to give others the benefit of the doubt because I knew there were going to be times that I would need the benefit of the doubt extended to me. There were still other times that Vincent annoyed me, just as there were times that I annoyed him; but we learned to talk and laugh about it because we both realized that because we were human, we were going to have those times.

One evening, I was home wondering what we were going to have for dinner because we did not have enough food in the house and we did not have money to buy anything to eat. Our finances had become that constricted. I called Vincent to let him know my dilemma and I say, "my" because I had never had that problem before. I never had to call him to let him know there was nothing to eat at home, because I always made sure that we had food in the house; but this time, I did not know what to do and I needed him to tell me. I called him at his job and said, "Bae, I don't know what we gon eat tonight. There is no food and there is no money."

Without hesitation, Vincent said, "Okay, Lo, put on a pot of rice and some beans."

I thought to myself, "I guess we'll have beans and rice tonight," because I was not expecting him to bring anything home. As he walked through the door smiling, I saw a box of Popeye's chicken in his hand. "How did you get that?" I asked, looking bewildered because I knew he did not have any money either. He did not say anything but he touched his chest. Not understanding what he meant by that, I asked again, "How did you get that cause you don't have no money?" Still smiling, he put his hand on his chest again and I noticed that his necklace was not there. "You pawned your necklace!" I said in astonishment.

"Yes," he said still smiling. Vincent had a gold necklace with an anchor on it that he had had for years and I had never known him to pawn anything; but when I saw the necklace gone, I knew that's what he had done.

At the time I did not understand what had come over me, but I was loving my husband like never before. "I love you!" I said. Walking up to him, I said it again, "I love you!" as I wrapped my arms around him and gave him a big kiss. I took the chicken and fixed dinner for us, still feeling an overwhelming sense of love for him. Later that night, I went to work and I just could not get over what had happened earlier. I told a couple of my coworkers about it while thanking and praising God and they praised Him with me. They might not have understood why I was praising God because after all, we did not have any money to get food to eat but that was not what I thought about. All I could think about was my husband's action of pawning his necklace to take care of me and the kids.

Later, I came to understand why I had renewed love for my husband. God had given me fresh eyes and showed me Vincent like I had never seen him before. I had never seen my husband as being a provider for our household because I never gave him a chance to do it. There was never a need for me to call him about not having any food or not having money to buy food because I always had it; but it was God who put us in that place and I had to call him. I know that if God had not done that, I would have missed the fullness of who and what my husband was to me and our household.

Eventually, our van was repossessed; but for me, it was a relief. A big weight was lifted off my shoulders because I no longer had to worry about how to make the payments on it. My pastor found out about the repossession and offered the church's help in catching up the payments. We thanked him but turned it down and I said to him, "I am so glad we don't have to worry about how we gon make them payments; we will be fine." Although I was relieved, I was also embarrassed to have the van repossessed because I was known to be on top of my game with finances; but during that time, I could not reconcile what was happening. We were paying our tithes and offerings, so God was supposed to make sure our bills would get paid and that we were taken care of; or at least that is what I thought. I was young in the Lord and did not understand His ways, but God was taking care of us; just not the way I expected Him to do it.

My husband was not bothered by what was going on. He always assured me that we were going to be fine. However, I was used to having enough to take care of myself and not depend on someone else, but that's not what God wanted for me. God showed me that I could depend on my husband to take care of us, and I learned to rest in that. We still had everything we needed, just not everything we wanted. My husband and I still had our jobs, but we had to cut back on our wants. It took some getting used to the adjustment of not having our van, but we did not skip a beat. That little two-door hatchback Honda took us everywhere we needed to go. We never missed a church service. Vincent, myself, our three kids, and my mother-in-law all loaded into that car and went to church. One day as we arrived at church and began to get out of the car one by one, a young girl said in amazement, "That's a cool car; they just keep on coming out of that little car!" We laughed because it was hilarious, but she was serious.

Sometime later, I believed God was impressing upon me to quit my job so I went to Vincent and said, "Vincent, I believe God is telling me to leave my job."

"Well, Lo, if that's what you believe God is telling you to do, then do it," he said. That was not the response I expected because we were already struggling with our finances. I had been at my place of employment for over ten years and my pay was more than his. I wanted to obey God but if Vincent had showed any concerns about me leaving my job, I don't think I would have left.

After putting in my two weeks' notice, I went to talk to the head of human resources. "What are you going to do?" she asked me.

"I don't know, but I believe God told me to leave so I'm leaving," I answered.

"I wish I was that bold," she responded which was surprising to me because she was the head of human resources. She was the person responsible for hiring and firing the employees but from her response, it seemed like she wanted to leave the company as well but was not bold enough to do so. Leaving the job for me meant over half the income of our household would be gone. It was not a bold move on my part, it was an obedient one. My employment was my security in continuing to orchestrate my life the way I wanted to. I just knew God had a better job in store for me so that I could continue to do that.

After two weeks, I left my job and immediately started looking for another one. I knew that whatever God had for me was greater than what I was leaving. Well, it was something greater, but not in the way I was expecting. The greater that God was doing was inwardly not outwardly. I began putting in applications at several businesses but did not get a job offer from any of them. I had a decent resume but no one would hire me. A friend of mine told me that the post office was hiring, so I applied for a job there and got it. However, it was for the third shift and after working one partial night, I quit. I went home and I said to Vincent, "I can't work that shift anymore. I forgot how tired I used to be working third shift."

"Well, don't go back, Lo. You don't have to work that shift."

I continued for some time applying for other jobs, but none came through for me;. and with over half the income gone out of our household, money got really tight. The bills kept coming and I did not know what bills to pay, how to pay them, or when to pay them. "Vincent, these are the bills that are due and this is how much we got. What bills do you want me to pay?" I asked him, knowing that the money was not enough to pay all the bills that were due.

Without hesitation, Vincent began giving me instructions as to what to do. "Lo, put this amount on that one and this amount on another one," he would say, and I did what he told me to do. He was doing his thing and it felt good. There was no hint of despair in his voice and for me it was liberating. Where had he been all those years? Well, he was always there; but me and my independent, self-sufficient mindset was in his way. God was showing me who my husband was and I liked him. God was also changing me so that I could receive the love He had for me through my husband. It was refreshing to know I could depend on Vincent to take care of us. God let me see that the weight I was carrying, thinking that I had to keep it all together, was not for me to carry and that I could give it to Vincent because he could handle it.

Although our finances were tight, I was relieved beyond measure of not having to worry about what to do and how to do it. God shifted that responsibility to my husband where it belonged, and it felt good. I am forever thankful that God did not show me that it would be four years before I would work again because if I had known that, I would never have left my job. But because I expected something greater in the way of a job and Vincent told me to leave if that's what I believed God was telling me to do, there was no hesitation in my mind about leaving the job. I did not know what God was doing, but never in a million years did I expect to become a housewife and depend on my husband to take care of us. God showed me that I had a husband, not just a man; and my respect and honor for him as my husband increased exponentially.

Taking the responsibility of managing our household was new to Vincent, and sometimes he made decisions that I did not think were in our best interest. After voicing my opinion, I left the decision up to him. Sometimes the results of his decisions seemed to be less than favorable, but God tempered me. Instead of berating him for making a decision that did not produce the best results by saying things such as, "See, if you had listened to me, this wouldn't have happened." Instead, I would say, "It's alright, bae, we'll be fine." That was to let him know we were in this together and I trusted his decision making. I did not want it back on me. When he saw that I trusted him, he began to ask for my opinion in the decision making.

Still, there were times when Vincent's attitude frustrated me since he had more say in managing our household and I know at times my attitude frustrated him. God was transforming my mind and it didn't happen overnight. We often bumped heads in that arena. "I'm the man of the house," was coming out of his mouth a little too often for me.

I would say, "You don't have to tell me you're the man of the house, just be the man of the house." Because we did not get marriage counseling to foreknow what was in store for us, we learned by trial and terror. The key word there is 'learned' because I did not know how to be a wife just as Vincent did not know how to be a husband. God taught us; we were in His marriage class and did not even know it. Thankfully, we submitted ourselves to God so that we could be taught of Him. We did not realize God was using our marriage to refine us and get rid of the impurities we learned in our upbringing from the homes we were raised in and from society, and it did not always feel good. God was making us to be the husband and wife we needed to be to each other. God brought order into our home. He helped me to get rid of that independent mindset and transformed my mind to be Vincent's wife and in doing so, Vincent did not have to engage in battle to be the husband he needed to be in our marriage. God did that for him because it was God who checked me when I got out of line.

Although we lost tangible possessions, the wisdom and knowledge we gained were invaluable. I remember saying to Vincent, "I wanna be like an ornament for you. I wanna make you look good," because that's what God had done in my heart. When I said it, I didn't think about the scriptures at 1 Peter 3:4 that says, *"But let it be the hidden man of the heart, in that which is not corruptible, even the ornament of a meek and quiet spirit."* I'm sure I had read it before, but when I read it again, I thought, "This is what God has done in me." It was not about my appearance such as clothes, hair, or jewelry because jeans and a t-shirt were still what I liked wearing most. It was the hidden man of the heart that God had changed, and that's what others saw in our marriage. I absolutely loved being Vincent's wife and I wanted to represent him wherever I went. I would rather have been with him than any other person because he became my best friend. We relished being with each other because we allowed each other to be ourselves. God had showed us that we could not change ourselves, much less anyone else; so we learned to accept and respect each other for who God had created us to be. No, we were not perfect, but that is the beauty in relationship: how God brings two imperfect people together and He is still glorified in the midst.

While shopping at Wal-mart shopping, a guy who visited our church sometimes walked up to us and asked, "Have y'all seen the movie Fireproof?"

"No," we both answered.

"Y'all need to see that movie because when I saw it, I thought about y'all. Y'all have the perfect marriage," he said. We knew the gentleman but had not spent a significant amount of time in his presence, so we were surprised by his comment but thankful. It was an awkward moment, because the most we had said to him was hello and that is what we were expecting to happen that time as well. But he stopped us to tell us what he thought of our marriage.

Also, ladies would often stop us in the store and ask, "How do you get him to come to the store with you?"

My response would be, "Because he wants to come with me; I don't have to do anything to get him to come to the store with me." Time together was not a luxury that we had an abundance of, so that was more time together for us. Although after leaving the store, I sometimes wished he had stayed home; because whenever he came to the store with me, we usually spent more money than I had intended.

Chapter 7

Marriage Is Perfect

As Vincent and I continued to grow in God's grace, our love for God grew and so did our love for each other; we began to experience mature love. Early on in our marriage, one of Vincent's biggest frustrations with me was not enough lovemaking. Vincent was young and full of vigor; I say 'young' because he was four years younger than me. I called him the energizer bunny because he could go on and on and on, and that was in any kind of physical activity. He often played basketball with our boys, his nephews and their friends who were much younger than him and he would always come home and say, "Guess who won," with a victory grin on his face or flexing his muscles because he always won. That same energy carried over into his desire to make love but sometimes I just wanted to sleep, especially when I was working the third shift. "Lo, you're beautiful and I enjoy making love to you," he said.

"I enjoy making love to you too, but I can't help it if I fall asleep," I responded.

"You just wanna control when we make love," he said. I did not think of it as controlling at first but as I thought about it, it was in way because I knew that if I wanted to make love, he was always ready; but that was not always the case if he wanted to make love.

Since God had given me a husband with a high sex drive, He had to help me please him. One day I heard the Lord plainly say to me, "You need to exercise." I started walking around our neighborhood but it was a sporadic activity. I did not think I needed to exercise much because my weight was not a problem, so I thought walking every now and then was sufficient. After our van was repossessed, I could no longer take Vincent Jr. to school. I had to walk him to catch the bus. Again, I clearly heard the Lord say, "Now you can exercise," so I started walking every morning after our son boarded the bus for school. Obviously, the sporadic walking was not what the Lord had in mind. After doing that for a while, I started working out using workout DVDs, and the exercising gave me more energy to keep up with my energetic husband in the bedroom. I'm not sure if that's why God told me that I needed to exercise, but it sure did help.

Vincent taught me how to really enjoy our lovemaking. I thought I had enjoyed lovemaking in the past, but it was not until one evening as Vincent and I were lying in bed after making love that it took on a whole new meaning to me. "Lo are you satisfied?" Vincent asked. I was not a virgin when my husband and I began seeing each other and I had been with a few guys. However, not one of them had ever asked me whether I was satisfied after sex. In fact, I never thought about my satisfaction. Sex for me was not about me being satisfied, it was about satisfying the man and giving him what he wanted. Since no one had ever asked me about my sexual satisfaction before, that is how I thought it was supposed to be.

Before my husband, I thought sex was letting the man do what he wanted and then acting like I was satisfied. During sex, I moaned a little and when my partner was about to have an orgasm, I followed his movement and his quick breathing; when he finished, I was finished. That's what I thought sex was because that's what my sexual experiences were until I met Vincent; he changed that for me with that one simple question to which I responded, "Yeah, I enjoyed it."

"But did you come?" he plainly asked me.

I was not sure how I should answer that question. I wanted to lie and say, "Yes I came," because I did not want to bruise his ego; but my answer was, "Well, no, but it was good."

"Lo, I climax every time we have sex and I want you to climax just like I do," he said. Well, his ego was not bruised and 'good' was not good enough for him. We began to have mature discussions about our sexual relationship and before long, I no longer had to fake orgasms; I began having real orgasms. Vincent made my sexual satisfaction a priority. He taught me how to ask for what I wanted, when I wanted it, and how I wanted it because he wanted me to enjoy our lovemaking just as much as he did.

"Vincent, you make me feel like a virgin, like there has never been anyone but you," I said to him. No one had ever loved me with the pure, unselfish, unfeigned love that Vincent loved me with. He did not approach our lovemaking to just get what he wanted; it was about what he could give me, which was pure and unadulterated love. That love put me in an entirely different headspace when it came to making love to my husband and I wanted more of it. That is the love God gave him to love me with and God transformed me so that I could receive it.

In our earlier years when God was taking me through the transformation process of making me Vincent's wife, I needed a little help to get in the mood to make love. During those times, I was easily annoyed by him as I'm sure he was annoyed with me, but that didn't take away his desire to make love. I needed help to make love when I was annoyed with him. In my desire to please God, I knew that I had to please my husband too. So sometimes to get in the mood, I had to find a place to spend a few minutes of alone time with God before going to bed where I knew Vincent was waiting for me. Then afterwards, I was eager to join my husband in our bed for some passionate lovemaking. Vincent did not like me coming to bed a little later than him but when he saw that I was ready for him, he was fine with it. Eventually, God matured me to not have to spend those few minutes with Him to get in the mood for making love with my husband. Other times, I'd play romantic music and light candles to enhance the mood.

When Vincent understood that I needed a little help getting in the mood, he would already have the candles lit and the music playing when I came to bed, which made me want him even more because he showed me that he cared about what I needed and wanted. I enjoyed foreplay such as talking, kissing, and caressing. Vincent did not need much of that, but he learned to slow it down and give me more foreplay. We began to talk more about lovemaking and what we wanted from each other. Then we began to talk more during lovemaking and oh, my! "It's all worth it," I said to him one night after our lovemaking.

"What's all worth it?" he asked.

"This makes it worth putting up with you all day," I said, and we both laughed. Making love was a nightcap that we both needed and enjoyed regularly, and it kept the sweetness in our marriage. After all the things we both had to encounter in a day (whether from family, coworkers, or church members), our nightcap together gave us something to look forward to at the end of the day.

Making love with my husband was an aspect of my worship to God because I realized that not only did my husband want to make love to me, but he needed to make love to me. He needed to release his strength and God knew that; that is why He gave us marriage. I wanted all his strength, and I did not want him to share his strength with another woman. To feel his strength released in me was so fulfilling because I knew I was not only giving him what he wanted, but I was giving him what he needed. Listening to the infrequency of lovemaking by some married couples was unthinkable to me. I heard someone say that they make love maybe four times a month and I could not imagine that. If me and my husband went more than two days without making love, he would become irritable and not fun to be around.

"You get grumpy if we go longer than two days without making love," I told him. I do not even think he noticed it, but he would get short with responses, and he did not laugh and joke as much. "Oh, I know what you need and I got you," I would say to him. After we made love, he was back to his friendly, joking self again. For several years, I snuggled in his arm and laid my head on his chest every night as we lay in bed and if we had not already made love, the result from feeling the heat of our bodies touching usually led to lovemaking. I wanted him to know that I was ready for whatever he wanted to do; the caressing would start by him or me, which led to kissing, and then to us making love. I was ready to give my husband what he needed and in turn, I got what I needed, not just in the bed, but all day long.

Because of what he saw in our marriage, our pastor came to us and asked if we would be over the married couple's ministry. As I thought about it, it was ironic as he was the same pastor who would not perform our wedding ceremony because we could not take his required marriage counseling course. But God had plans for us to take His marriage course and the results of His lessons were evident. Our pastor believed we could help other married couples and we agreed to do it. The ministry included us teaching a ten-week course for couples engaged to be married and planning events for the married couples. We called it, "Marriage Is Perfect," knowing that statement is in total contrast to how most married couples would describe marriage.

We believed that God ordained marriage when he gave Eve to Adam. God's works are perfect and therefore, marriage is perfect. The problems come when we, the imperfect humans, partake in it. We wanted to put the blame for failing or failed marriages where it belongs, which is on us. We knew that no one's marriage was perfect in the sense of never having a problem but with God's help, we could work through our imperfections and have a marriage that's pleasing to Him. None of us are perfect but we wanted others to know that even with our imperfections, marriage can be perfect in Christ Jesus.

Vincent and I knew God had given us something special in our marriage and we wanted to share what He had given us with other married couples in the hope that they would experience God's perfect marriage too. Also, we wanted to bring in a fresh wind of positive and encouraging energy to marital conversations. It was disheartening for us to hear the negative connotations at the mention of marriage, especially in the church. We were so excited about what God was doing and had done in our marriage. And because we were members of the church and we all had the same access to God, Vincent and I were under the persuasion that church should have been the one place where marriage was spoken of in a positive way. It was our desire to change the negative narrative about marriage.

By this time, I had started working at the church part time; our pastor asked me to take a receptionist position. Initially, I did not want to work at the church because I knew my pastor was a prudent man and I did not think I was up to par. I told my husband I did not want to work there because I did not think I was sufficient. Then while praying one morning, I heard the Lord say, "Iron sharpens iron," but I only considered my pastor to be iron and not myself.

Vincent said, "Lo, you are iron, so you sharpen him too." He opened my eyes to what the Lord was saying to me. Just as I would be better from working with him, he would also be better from working with me; we were going to sharpen each other. For some reason, we put pastors and those who are behind the pulpit on pedestals like they are not human; and if we are not careful, they become a god to us. Pastors do not know everything and they do not have all the answers. I believe that working at the church with my pastor allowed me to see that he was just as human as we all are, and I stopped looking to him for answers and sought God more for understanding and wisdom.

Working at the church also gave me access to books and time to assemble the teaching material for Marriage Is Perfect. My pastor gave us books and we purchased books on our own. Once we started reading the books, we realized that although we did not take marriage classes before our marriage, God had given us marriage classes during our marriage, and we were able to use our own experiences to teach each class. We did not want to only give information; we wanted to use our experiences to show others that marriage does work if we do what God tells us to do. We brought those taking the classes into our marriage and talked about what we had to endure to have the marriage we had.

After assembling the teaching materials, which Vincent left up to me, we began teaching the Marriage Is Perfect classes to engaged couples. We both discovered that teaching and sharing what God had done in our marriage with others was so rewarding. There was a chapter in the teaching materials about the three stages of marriage: enchantment, disenchantment, and maturity, and we shared our feelings and actions during the different stages. For example, for the first two years of our marriage, we seemed to have adjusted from living together to married life seamlessly and did not start to experience resistance until after we were both saved. We thought that since we had done the right thing and gotten married, it was only going to get better from there; it did but just not the way we thought it would. I would not call it the enchantment stage because we had lived together for seven years so the enchantment stage for us was not long at all.

The disenchantment stage started quickly for us. That's when I realized that Vincent was not my problem, but the problem was me. When God began to mold me into the wife He wanted me to be, I blamed Vincent for my discomfort in the process that God was taking me through. I became disenchanted with him and was easily irritated by the little things he did. Because of my lack of being able to express myself at that time, I did not always share my feelings with him and the frustration built. But when I did begin to share how I felt, he became defensive, which did not make it easy for me because I do not like to argue. "I am not trying to start an argument, I just want to tell you how I feel," I would say to him. So when I made a change and began to share my feelings, he also had to make a change because he was not used to it.

"When she changed, I had to change as well; I had to change for the change," he shared with the class. Ultimately, he stopped being defensive and he started listening to me, which was great because I did not necessarily need a response, I just needed to know he was hearing me. Then sometimes he would come back later and say, "Lo, you're right and I'm sorry," or we would discuss it further. That was the beginning of our friendship because there is no friendship if one person in the relationship cannot express to the other his or her feelings.

One day at a church service, the pastor asked how many of the husbands were bold enough to ask their wives, 'Would you marry me again?' Vincent, being the confident man that he was, asked me the question when we got home and to his surprise, "No, I wouldn't," was my response because that was how I felt at that time. It was not easy for me to say that to him, but I had to be truthful.

When sharing that in the class Vincent said, "I asked her with my chest out because I just knew her answer was gonna be yes. When she said no, I felt like someone had hit me in my chest, but it did not discourage me; what it did was give me a target in prayer because I wanted to be the best husband I could be to her."

Eventually, we got through the disenchantment stage and went on to the maturity stage, which was what I called the 'smooth sailing stage.' In this stage, we did not hold grudges and we were quick to say, "I'm sorry, forgive me, I was wrong," even if we did not think the other one should have been offended because we both knew we came up short sometimes and must extend forgiveness to receive it. I was so thankful that my husband still loved me with all of my shortcomings. We came to a place in our marriage where we laughed at our shortcomings instead of holding them against each other, as long as there was no infidelity or disrespect.

Mostly, the problem was that we did not accept each other for who God created us to be and we tried to recreate each other into what we wanted (like God did not know what He was doing when He created us). All marriages go through the same thing because you have two unique individuals who are becoming one. The problem is that most marriages do not get through the disenchantment stage because they do not have someone to tell them that it is normal and that healthy marriages will go through it and get through it. In fact, we told the couples if they were not going through uncomfortable times in their marriage, then they were not doing something right. We let them know it was not easy but with God, all things are possible.

The first event that Vincent and I planned for the couples was a two-day conference from Friday night to Saturday morning. The first night of the event consisted of dinner and karaoke. At that time, there was not much R&B heard or sung around church folks. We knew what we had planned was unconventional for a church event, but we felt it was very much needed for married couples. We wanted it to be a fun, let your hair down, no suits please, type of event, and it was. Before we started the karaoke segment, we passed the song list around to recruit couples to sing, especially our pastor and his wife; we knew that by them participating, it would encourage others to participate as well and it did.

My husband and I went first because we wanted to break the ice. Vincent could not hold a tune at all but he was entirely in when having fun. The song we chose to sing was 'Cruisin' by Smokey Robinson. Vincent sang loudly and off key while I swayed to the music saying, "Sing it, baby," because it was all in having fun. We wanted others to know it was not about displaying anyone's voice, we just wanted to have a good time. After some coaxing, we had about ten couples volunteer to participate in the karaoke. We were having an enjoyable time but there were about thirty couples at the event, so we also had quite a few that did not volunteer for the karaoke.

After the couples were done with their chosen songs, it was still early and the ambience was high with laughter and fun, so I asked all the women if they wanted to sing a song to the husbands. Almost all the women came up and we sang, "You Don't Have to Be a Star" by Marilyn McCoo and Billy Davis Jr. Then Vincent did the same thing with the men, and most of them came up as well to sing, "I Heard It Through the Grapevine" by Marvin Gaye. Still, it saddened me that most of the people wanted to sing, but just not with their spouse. In former days, church was extra rigid with rules and regulations of what we could and could not do, even to the point of taking the fun out of marriages. It was our desire to show the married couples how we enjoy each other and hopefully inspire them to find ways to enjoy each other.

The last day of the conference on the following Saturday morning, Vincent and I shared what God had done in our marriage. Then our pastor shared some insightful nuggets with us. That was our first event with the married and engaged couples, and we were so thankful for the enthusiasm and encouraging remarks we received from those in attendance such as, "It was perfect; we had fun on Friday night and then Saturday morning we were fed some good food from the teaching."

Some people wondered if what they saw in our marriage was real. I've heard married people broadcast how much they love their spouses and brag about how they treat each other, what things they purchase for each other, or how much money they spend on each other. When I hear that kind of talk, that's all it is to me, talk because I believe the only person who needs to know how much I love him is my spouse; and if I show him and tell him, there is no need to prove it to anyone else. Vincent and I did not have to say how much we loved each other or brag about what we do for each other publicly. We showed and told each other often so when we were out among others, what we did in private showed in public without either one of us opening our mouth. People saw the genuineness and purity of our love and commitment to each other, so we did not have to talk about it. We let them know it was real and, "What you see is what it is." That is what God did in us and for us.

Chapter 8

Restoration: A Father and His Son

While God was processing us for His perfect marriage, he was also restoring Vincent's relationship with his father because when Vincent and I first met, they didn't have one. In fact, he said he had not spoken to his father since he and Victor left home to go to college: "Me and Victor got accepted to Bethune Cookman so we left Rochester the same day we graduated, and my father didn't even come to our graduation. My mom came but not our father. Lo, I hate my father," is what he would say to express how he felt about him.

"You can't hate your father; how can you hate your father?" I asked him. Although I had not seen or talked to my father in almost twenty years when Vincent and I met, I did not hate him so that was incomprehensible to me. Also, when he said it, I did not hear hate in his voice. I heard it as if he did not know what else to feel.

"Lo, my pop was abusive to my mom and he abused us. He used to make us sit on the floor and beat us across our heads with a belt for punishment," he said. Instantly, my imagination went there and I saw them crouching on the floor, trying to cover their heads with their arms while their father whacked them this way and that way; that was harsh punishment to me. Don't get me wrong, I do not have a problem with whippings because I got my share growing up and I know that in today's time, some would consider it abuse. However, the whippings I received at the hands of my mother and my older siblings kept me out of a lot of mischief and I am thankful for them. Nonetheless, to hear my husband talk about the whippings and punishments that he and his siblings received from the hands of their father, it was abuse. "My father was so mean, he used to make us pick the lint balls from the carpet for punishment," he said. He went on to ask, "Who makes their kids pick little pieces of cotton off the carpet?"

I heard one of his sisters say, "Buddy Boy used to come home and beat everybody from the wife on down to the children." Vincent's father's name was Jesse Paige but they called him Buddy Boy.

"Lo, if we had a cold, we could not even cough because he said we were making too much noise. 'Stop making all that noise up there,'" is what he said his father would say if he heard one of them coughing. "So whenever any of us had to cough, we had to go to the bathroom and flush the toilet while we coughed so Pop would not hear us." He also told me of another time that he was playing outside and broke his arm but he did not tell his father, fearing he would whip him. His siblings tried to quietly help him upstairs past their father so he would not find out, but one of the stairs was loose and it creaked whenever someone stepped on it. "'Who's that going up them stairs?'" he said his father asked when he heard the creak from the stairs. "Me," Vincent responded, trying to sound normal, but he was crying because he was in so much pain and terrified of his father finding out. He went days without his father knowing of his condition. Eventually, his father did find out and he was upset, but he did not whip him for it.

On another occasion, Vincent's father was physically abusing his mom and his oldest brother Tony ran into the kitchen where he was abusing her. "Tony grabbed him and threw him up against the refrigerator and Pop couldn't get loose. Tony held him and said some words to him and when he let him go, Tony ran out of the house. Tony came home and the next morning, Pop woke him up with a knife pointed at his neck saying, 'I could've killed you if I wanted to. Get your stuff and get out of here and don't you ever come back.' Tony sat up, put his clothes on while watching Pop the whole time and he left the house and never came back. Victor and I could not wait to leave after graduation to get away from the craziness." I understood why he had feelings of resentment toward his father because he witnessed and experienced some harsh times in their home, but I still do not think he ever really hated him.

His father called Victor 'K1' and he called Vincent 'K2.' Vincent said he never knew why he called them by those names, especially since Vincent was the oldest (he thought he should've been called K1). The other siblings said Buddy Boy favored the twins and took them everywhere. "They thought we were having fun when we went with Pop, but we were not having fun," Vincent said. "Pop would take us with him and we had to sit in the car sometimes for hours and wait while Pop went inside the home he was visiting. We could not even get out to go to the bathroom. Sometimes he would bring snacks out to the car for us to eat, but they were not fun times." "One time, he took me and Victor with him and left us at a lady's house while he went somewhere. While we were there, me and Victor were sitting on the floor and the lady came and sat right in front of us with her legs wide open and she was not wearing any underwear. Me and Victor looked at each other to see if the other one saw what was in front of us. We did not want to look but we could not help it. Now here me and Victor were, we might have been ten years old, and we had to sit and watch her until she thought it was enough. That lady knew exactly what she was doing sitting in front of us like that." Although the other siblings thought it was favoritism that Vincent and Victor received from their father, Vincent did not see it like that. "It's not like we had good times when we went with him, so it was more like punishment to us."

Vincent's father was a crossing guard for the schools in the county in which they lived and according to Vincent, the kids loved him. The other kids did not believe that the nice man who stopped traffic for them to cross the street could be the same man who was so mean to his own children. They did not see the alcoholic who came home every night and sat in the car for several minutes before coming inside, looking for a reason to be angry with his wife and his children so he could get violent with them. But the other kids did know that they were not permitted to come to their home to play. Their father only allowed a select few to come to their house, their cousins Kevin and David (who were closer in age to them) and an older cousin named Jody.

My sister Jonita lived in Long Island and one summer before we were married, we went to visit her. At the time, Victor was living in The Bronx, which was thirty minutes or so from where Jonita lived, so we were able to visit them both. During our visit, Vincent and Victor made plans to visit their father in Rochester. Neither one of them had seen him since they had graduated from high school. Vincent Jr. was about two years old at the time and Vincent wanted to take him with them to see his father. They visited with their father and their brothers Dale and Eric who were still living in Rochester as well. From what they told me, the visit was great, and their father was happy to see them. The initial plan was to spend one night in Rochester but the drive was much longer than they expected, so they stayed for two nights. After visiting for two nights in Rochester, they returned to Long Island. I saw the joy Vincent had of seeing his father again and that he did not really hate his father. He just did not have many opportunities to enjoy his father growing up; but during their visit, he got the chance. This started the restoration of their relationship.

The church my husband and I attended taught about the father-son relationship. The teaching inspired Vincent and I to value our relationships with our own fathers. As a result, he started calling his father at least once a month. In the phone conversations with his father, Vincent never made mention of the past as to the abuse he, his siblings, or his mother received. Their conversations were always pleasant and Vincent ended the conversations with, "Pop, I love you." At first, his father did not reciprocate the response with an "'I love you too,'" but that did not stop Vincent from ending the conversations the same way each time. Eventually, his father responded, "'I love you too son.'" "Lo, I have never heard my father say he love me until now." The phone conversations continued and soon his father started sending birthday and holiday greeting cards. Vincent did the same to him and their relationship flourished.

One year while planning our summer road trip, we chose Rochester as one of our destinations. We so enjoyed our road trips and each summer we planned one with at least two or three destinations. We also made sure to visit my father in Alabama as well. Vincent wanted me to meet his father and I wanted to meet him, but there was uneasiness in doing so because of the horror stories I heard about Buddy Boy. I did not know what to expect. To my surprise, he was a pleasurable man. When we got to Rochester, we went to Dale's house. He told us about a store that Buddy Boy was working at and we found him there. Vincent and Vincent Jr. went inside to get him while Fantasy and I waited in the car. Buddy Boy came out of the store grinning and we got out of the car as Vincent introduced him to us. After talking and laughing for a few minutes, Buddy Boy said he had to get back to work so he told Vincent to come by his apartment later when he was off and that is what we did. He was the antithesis of the stories I had heard about him. Instead of being an unstable and sometimes violent alcoholic, I had the pleasure of meeting a jovial gentleman who was happy to see his son and his son's family.

Later that evening, we went to Buddy Boy's apartment. He lived in a senior housing complex. As we walked into his apartment, I was surprised by the warm, homey feeling I felt. The walls and shelves were decked with pictures of Vincent and his siblings when they were younger as well as pictures of his grandchildren whom he had never met in person. There were also pictures of other family members and Vincent walked around and looked at the pictures asking, "Pop, who is this?" when he saw someone that he did not know, and Buddy Boy let him know who was in the pictures. Vincent and his father talked and laughed for a while. I learned that he knew my mom and one of my uncles.

As we were preparing to leave for the evening, Buddy Boy came out with a camera in his hand. "This is for you," he said as he handed the camera to Fantasy.

"Thank you," she said.

Then he said to me, "And this is for you," as he handed me a wooden carved African mask.

"Oh, okay, thank you," I said as I took the mask. He also gave Vincent Jr. a toy box that vibrated and said, "'Excuse me, excuse me, can you get me out of here?'" It was something small but it was hilarious because it sounded as if there was a little man inside the box wanting to get out. When we got in the car, Vincent and I found it strange and funny that his father had given me the mask. "I didn't know what to say when he gave me the mask," I said to Vincent. "That's why I just said 'Oh, Okay, thank you.'"

"He just wanted to give y'all something," Vincent said. The man I met was nothing like the stories I had heard of him. He was one of the most pleasant people I had ever met, and it was a joy to meet him. After our visit, Vincent and I made it a priority to go to Rochester every other year to visit his father and other family members.

One day, Vincent's cousin who lived in Buffalo called him and said, "You need to come see about your father." "Your father is here in Buffalo in the hospital, and you all need to come see about him." Buddy Boy didn't have a good relationship with any of his other kids and he did not call Vincent when he fell ill, so Vincent did not know. In fact, he did not call any of his children to let them know of his illness. Eventually, he got better and was able to go home. Unfortunately, he was diagnosed with prostate cancer and was in and out of the hospital. The cancer got worse and metastasized to his bones and it became difficult for him to live independently of help from someone else. He had a friend who came to his apartment daily and helped him out tremendously with his daily activities.

Vincent continued with the phone calls to check on his father: "Hey, Pop, how ya doing?" "Hello, son, I'm doing good," was always Buddy Boy's answer. Vincent did not mention anything about the cancer or his health and they would go on talking. But Buddy Boy was not doing good; his health was declining.

The time came for another road trip with one of our stops being Rochester. That year, Victor and his daughter Sibel were here visiting from Turkey. Victor's residing in Turkey came about because when he lived here in the states, he met and married a woman from Turkey and they had a daughter together. His wife went home to Turkey for a visit with her family and she took their daughter with her. It was Victor's understanding that she would return to the states after the visit, but she decided to stay to be near her family. Not long after that, Victor informed us that he was quitting his job and moving to Turkey. Vincent and I thought Victor's decision was radical because he was moving to a foreign country without a job and without the skill to speak or understand the language. Nevertheless, that is what he was willing to do to be with his family.

Victor began teaching private English lessons and later got a job as an English teacher at a private school. He also learned to speak and understand enough of the language to live in the country. A couple of years later, Victor and his wife divorced but he decided to remain in Turkey so he could be in his daughter's life. Being a teacher in Turkey made it possible for Victor to take extended vacations in the summer. Whenever he and Sibel came for vacation, they stayed for at least two months and Vincent would start planning for their visit early in the year.

We also invited our nephew Richard and his girlfriend Teal to come along on the road trip with us. We thoroughly enjoyed our road trips and for that one, Rochester was our first destination. From Sanford to Rochester is at least twenty-one hours driving straight through, which Vincent used to do when he was younger. But as we got older, he stopped driving straight through to our destinations if it was more than twelve hours because those long rides had become uncomfortable for both of us. Our plan was to drive twelve hours, rent a hotel room for the night, then get up the following morning to continue the trip.

We left early on a Saturday morning about seven o'clock in two cars. Vincent, me, and Vincent Jr. were in our car and Victor, Sibel, Richard, and Teal rented a car for the road trip. By this time, Delrick was married to his wife Tamika and had made us doting grandparents to three beautiful girls and Fantasy had moved into her own place, so they did not go with us. Vincent laid down his road trip rule before we left: "Alright, we're stopping about every four hours for bathroom, gas, and food break, so don't drink a lot between stops." He held to his rule. It was not a problem for Victor and the others because they knew Vincent and that he meant what he said. Victor called him Sergeant Paige because Vincent was a stickler for leaving and arriving on time and if that did not happen, it was because of something out of his control. With luggage loaded in the vehicles, Trip Tik Travel Planner in hand from AAA, and snacks, we hit the road. Hotels were reserved for each of our destinations, including the twelve-hour stop before we arrived in Rochester.

For our first stop, we only reserved one room for the seven of us because we only wanted to rest and freshen up before we did the remainder of the trip the following morning. "I got first dibs on the bathroom," I said as we arrived at the hotel. I had to call first dibs because there was only one bathroom and one shower and I could not wait. Then the others started calling out who was next to the bathroom. We all laughed as we headed to the hotel room. There were two beds and a chair in the room, so we slept where we could. If my memory serves me correctly, Vincent and I were in one bed, Teal and Sibel were in the other one, Victor slept in the chair and Richard and Vincent Jr. slept on the floor. It was only for one night, it was doable, and we made it happen. I loved it because those times make great memories to talk and laugh about later, which we did.

After waking and freshening up the following morning, we were on the road again headed for Rochester, which according to our Trip Tik, was another nine hours or so. When we arrived in Rochester, Vincent called his brother Dale and learned that his father was in the hospital so that was our first stop. "Me and Victor will go in first to let Pop know y'all are out here," Vincent said, and we agreed. About twenty minutes later, they came out and said, "Pop don't want to see nobody."

"Man, we done came all this way to see him and he don't want to see us?" Richard said indignantly. "Naw, I want to see him." Richard had never seen his grandfather and he did not want to leave Rochester without seeing him.

"We'll go talk to him again," Vincent said. Vincent and Victor went back in to talk to him and after a few minutes, they came to get us because Buddy Boy agreed to see us. Walking into the room, I did not know what to expect because he initially said he did not want to see anybody. However, he was his usual jovial self, talking to us all and laughing.

"Good, googly, moogly," Buddy Boy said when Richard introduced his girlfriend Teal to him, which meant that he thought she was very pretty. We all laughed and continued talking and laughing for the duration of our short visit with him.

We were only in Rochester for two nights and the following day, we went to Niagara Falls, which was a forty-five-minute drive from

Rochester. Vincent and Victor also took us to their childhood home and a park where they learned to play basketball. We also ran up and down a hill they called Big Bertha. They said when it used to snow, they used big pieces of cardboard to slide down the hill. Also, we visited one of their childhood friends who they called "Six-Nine" (because that is about how tall he was) before returning to our hotel rooms to prepare to leave the following morning. "Pop didn't want y'all to see him sick like that," Vincent said. "That's why he said he didn't want to see nobody." We were all so thankful that we did get a chance to see Buddy Boy while we were there.

The remainder of our vacation was amazing! It was one of the best road trips we had ever taken, stopping in New York City where we hopped on and off the subways, visited Madison Square Gardens, Ground Zero where the Twin Towers once stood, the Empire State Building, and other landmarks. Then we headed to Washington DC and visited the landmarks there before heading back home.

When we got home, Vincent continued to call his father to check on him and his father always said he was doing fine. About six months later, Buddy Boy's friend called Vincent and told him his father could no longer walk because the cancer had taken a toll on his bones and the care that he needed was too much for her to give. Buddy Boy knew he was not getting any better and he decided that a nursing home would be the best place for him to get the care he needed at that stage in his sickness. He was not able to walk and take care of his basic needs, so he needed Vincent to help him get his affairs in order and be there with him when he went to the nursing home. Buddy Boy had previously made the arrangements to go into the nursing home and he only had a couple of days to clear out his apartment before leaving. Vincent knew he had to be there for his father, so he immediately began planning to go to Rochester and asked me to come with him. Of course, I said yes; and a couple of days later, we were on a flight headed to Rochester.

Dale picked us up from the airport and took us to his father's apartment. Upon arrival, I went into the bedroom and greeted Buddy Boy because he was in bed, and we laughed and talked for a few minutes. After I greeted him, I went to the living room and Vincent began taking care of his father as I watched the television. He came in the living room several times and asked, "Lo, you alright?" "

Yes," I answered until I got hungry. Buddy Boy let Vincent use his car and we went out for something to eat. We had not made any arrangements for hotels or transportation for our stay in Rochester and once Vincent saw his father and the help he needed, he wanted to stay at the apartment with him. Vincent took me to a restaurant in downtown Rochester and we sat and ate.

"Lo, I want to stay with Pop tonight because he don't need to be there by himself."

"Okay, but I need to go to the store to get us some towels, some pillows and pillowcases," I said because I was not sure if there were any at his father's apartment. It is my practice to always take my own washcloths and soap with us when we stay at hotels. I was not sure if Buddy Boy had clean towels at the apartment, so before we went back, we went to Walmart and grabbed what we needed for our stay. I did not know where we were going to sleep because there was only one bed in the house and Buddy Boy was in that one. The only thing left to sleep on was the couch or the floor and I do not sleep comfortably on either; but I did not say anything because Vincent had enough on his mind taking care of his father. I don't know how we did it, but we both slept on the couch; his head was on one end and mine was on the other. It was not comfortable at all, but we made it work.

The following morning, Vincent and his father went out to take care of his father's business before he left to go to the nursing home while I stayed at the apartment. Vincent had to assist his father in getting up, getting dressed, and getting breakfast before they went out; he did it all, not wanting any help from me. He wanted to be the one to take care of his father. Vincent went outside to warm up the car before they were ready to leave. He came back inside with a look of reluctance on his face and said, "Lo, the car won't crank because the battery is dead. I left the lights on last night and it killed the battery and now I gotta go in here and let Pop know."

Buddy Boy had a roadside assistance plan, so he had Vincent call, and someone came about forty-five minutes later to get the car started. Buddy Boy waited in the apartment with me while Vincent waited outside for the roadside assistance company to come out. "That boy left them lights on and killed the battery in my car. I ought to whip his a**," he said.

I thought to myself, "Naw, Buddy Boy, those days are over." That was the only time I saw a hint of the man my husband and his siblings grew up with. The roadside assistance finally came, got the car started, and Vincent and his father left.

When they returned, I told Vincent what his father said and he just laughed. Later that day, Vincent took me on a scenic walk around the neighborhood. "We used to live in that house right there," he said pointing to a two-story home across the street. "This used to be a park where we all gathered," he said pointing to an area that had been built up with new homes. It had snowed the night before and I am a Florida girl, so I did not want to stay out too long in the cold. Buddy Boy was going to the nursing home the following morning and Vincent helped him pack the items he needed to take with him. I know he had to have over fifty caps, and he wanted to take them all with him. "

Pop, can I take a few of them?" Vincent asked and his father let him. Later that night as we were getting ready for bed, Vincent came to me and said, "Lo, I have to change Pop, he did the number two."

"Do you need my help?" I asked.

"No, I got it," he said. I had never known Vincent to clean and change the diaper of an adult before, but he did it. Then about fifteen minutes later as I was getting ready to shower, he came in the bathroom where I was and whispered, "Lo, he done sh***ed again."

I started laughing and asked, "You got it or do you need me to help you this time?"

"I got it," he said and he changed him again.

When Buddy Boy saw me the next morning, he said, "That boy changed me just like I was a baby. I mean he did a good job too." I was so pleased with the way my husband was taking care of his father.

The medical transportation van came to get Buddy Boy to take him to the nursing home and he was ready to go. He rode in the van as we followed along in his car. When we arrived at the nursing home, they were awaiting his arrival and we waited with him until they got him settled in his room. Then Vincent and I went back to Buddy Boy's apartment and began packing his things because we had to have everything out of the apartment in two days. We took the bulk of his belongings to the local Goodwill and found some people to give his furnishings to including the bed and living room furniture. That night, we discovered that the couch was a pull-out sofa bed! "Lo, look, this is a pull-out bed," Vincent said.

"You mean to tell me we could've been sleeping in a bed for the last two nights?" I asked in astonishment.

"Yeah, but we didn't know," Vincent said. But I tell you what, we sure enjoyed that pull-out sofa bed for the next couple of nights.

It took us the entire two days to clear out the apartment, and some of Buddy Boy's belongings that Vincent knew he had for a while, he wanted to keep. We rented a minivan to have extra space to bring the things that Vincent wanted home with us. After saying our good-byes to Buddy Boy, we proceeded to hit the road back to Sanford.

I knew Buddy Boy had cancer and that the doctors did not expect him to get better, but I was not expecting to receive a call from the nursing home just one month later informing Vincent that his father was not going to be with us much longer and if he wanted to see him alive, then he needed to come as soon as possible. "I can't believe it," I said to Vincent. "He seemed to be so strong and full of life when we left, and now they're saying he has a couple of days to live." I could not believe he was dying.

Vincent wanted to go be with his father: "Nobody wants to die alone. Lo, I have to go."

The following day, Vincent caught a flight to Rochester. From the airport, he went directly to the nursing home. He called me and said, "Lo, when Pop saw me walk in his room, he said 'Thank you Jesus.'"

"How is he doing?" I asked.

"It's not gon be much longer, Lo; he's dying," Vincent said.

"Wow, I didn't think it would happen this soon," I said.

"I don't see any of Pop's caps here; somebody done took 'em," Vincent said.

"Probably some of the workers there," I said. Buddy Boy gave Vincent the keys to his car to go where he needed to go, but Vincent stayed the night at the nursing home with him. The following day, Buddy Boy's condition worsened and Vincent called his mom and his siblings. He told them that it would not be much longer and if they wanted to say something to him, now was the time and they did. Before the next morning, Vincent called and said, "Lo, he's gone."

"Really?" I said.

"Yeah, I watched him take his last breath," he said crying.

"Baby, I am so proud of you right now. The honor and love you showed to your father… I love you, Vincent," I said as I was starting to feel the heaviness in my heart. I was so thankful to God for what He had done in their relationship. To know that when I first met my husband, he said he hated his father and to now see the love he had and showed for his father was a thing of beauty; I know that God was the one who did that. Vincent did not start building a relationship with his father because he wanted something from him, he did it because he wanted to show love and honor to his father.

"The reason the rest of them can't have a relationship with Pop is because they want him to apologize for what he did, but I never brought up the past with Pop," Vincent said. "I didn't want or expect an apology; I just loved him for who he was to me, my father."

Two days later, Vincent Jr. and I caught a flight to Rochester to be with Vincent because he had to make funeral arrangements for his father. Vincent had a friend in Rochester who worked as a manager at a hotel there and she gave us a substantial discount for hotel rooms because in the coming days, Vincent's mom, his siblings, and some of his nephews arrived in Rochester for the funeral. Vincent was not familiar with mortuaries in the Rochester area to know which funeral home to call to plan for his father's service, so his cousins Jody and Noreen pointed him in the right direction. With their help, Vincent made plans for the funeral service for his father. All of Vincent's siblings were there except Victor (who was in Turkey) and Tony who at the time was not prepared to come. Victor penned some words that Vincent read at their father's service. The family came together and gave Buddy Boy a nice homegoing service.

"I just wish they would've done this while he was alive," Vincent said.

Chapter 9

Times of Celebration

Vincent and I decided to sell our home in Deltona after living there for almost ten years. We realized that we spent most of our time in Sanford and wanted to move back. "It seems like the only thing we do in Deltona, is sleep," I said to Vincent. On the weekdays we would wake up, go to work, come home, and on at least three of the evenings, we were back in Sanford for prayer, bible study and choir rehearsal. Likewise on the weekends, we were at youth service on Saturday and church services on Sunday. Not to mention that both of our families were in Sanford, so it made sense for us to move back, which is what we did. We sold the house and moved into an apartment complex.

In April of 2010, Vincent and I celebrated fifteen years of marriage by going on a seven-day cruise. Several years earlier, we were introduced to cruising by our pastor and his wife and it immediately became our preferred getaway for fun and relaxation. "Sister Paige, why don't you and Deacon Paige come go on a cruise with me and my wife?" our pastor asked. After informing Vincent of his request, he excitedly said yes and the planning began. While on our first cruise, we couldn't believe what we had been missing. Vincent and I thoroughly enjoyed ourselves getting off the ship at the ports of call, going to dinner and shows in the evenings, and then going to the club to get our dance on. Our pastor made a humorous comment about us when we returned from our cruise to some of the members of the church saying, "The deacons said they were going to the club," and we all laughed about it because that was not the norm for church deacons but we were not the normal church deacons. We believed in enjoying each other and if dancing was an activity that encouraged enjoyment (especially for married couples), then that should not be a problem with the church.

After that first cruise, we went on a cruise every year, but we had never taken a seven-day cruise. For our fifteen-year anniversary, we decided to splurge a little and take a longer cruise than we had previously, and we were excited about it. Our cruise was set to sail on a Sunday and the day before, we decided to play tennis, which was one of our favorite recreational activities to do together. Vincent was very athletic, and he was an avid basketball fan and player. I was somewhat athletic and an avid basketball fan, but I could not play well, so we wanted a sport that we could enjoy together. When we saw Venus and Serena Williams playing tennis on television, both Vincent and I became fans of them and the sport. We bought tennis racquets and balls and went to the tennis court to try and mimic what we saw the Williams sisters do and became decent at it.

The apartment we moved into happened to have a tennis court right in front of it. The Saturday before our cruise, we had been playing tennis for about 30 minutes when as I was running across court to return the ball, something snapped in my right leg. Immediately, I stopped because of the pain and I thought it was a severe injury. Out of frustration, I slammed the tennis racquet to the ground and limped off the court. While following behind me as I limped to our apartment, Vincent asked, "What happened?"

"I don't know but I felt something snap in my leg," I said. I wanted to go to the hospital to have my leg checked out, but I didn't want them to tell me it was an injury that would prevent us from going on our cruise, so I lay on the couch and Vincent brought me some ice to put on my leg.

"Girl, your leg got to be alright so we can go on our cruise," Vincent said.

"Oh, we are going on our cruise," I said, still not sure whether we were going or not because I did not know what was going on with my leg. "I believe I pulled a muscle going after the ball, but I'll be alright," I hoped.

Our son, Delrick, came to the house and saw me lying on the couch with my leg up. "What happened?" he asked.

"Your mother done pulled a muscle or something while we were playing tennis and we are supposed to be going on the cruise tomorrow," Vincent said pessimistically. "She knows she gettin' old," he said shaking his head. I was four years older than him and he often reminded me of the fact that I was his senior.

"You gon be able to go on the cruise?" Delrick asked.

"Oh, we are going on our cruise. I will be alright," I said definitively. I believed that until I tried to walk on that leg, then oh, the pain. Applying any amount of pressure on my leg caused it to hurt badly. I didn't know if I could do it but I was determined to go on our cruise the next day (pulled muscle and all), so I spent the evening icing and resting my leg.

The following morning, it was even more painful to walk on my injured leg but I got up and got dressed to board that ship for our cruise. Vincent had a small ace bandage at the house, and he helped me wrap my leg with it. Then about 7am, we left our apartment headed for the Port of Miami. The cruise ship was set to sail at 5pm and we had about a four-hour drive to Miami, but we wanted to get to the port around lunchtime because we knew that there was early boarding available. Upon arriving in Miami, I realized I needed a larger ace bandage for my leg because the small ace bandage did not give sufficient coverage and protection and I limped badly. Also, I believed my leg was vulnerable to further injury if it was not well covered and tightly wrapped, so we stopped at a Walgreen's and got a larger ace bandage that covered my entire calf and lower leg area. The larger bandage felt more secure for protection and it helped to ease the pain, but I still limped when I walked. I was not going to let the pain and the limp detract from the excitement I had of having that time away with my husband. I was ready to get on that ship for seven days of bliss with my best friend and lover. Once we boarded the ship, the anticipation of celebrating our anniversary was all I thought about and I didn't mind that I had to have my leg wrapped or walk with a limp to do it.

After checking in, we ate lunch, changed into some relaxing attire, and got into cruising mode. Usually, we participate in the dancing and festivities as the cruise ship sets sail but because of my leg, we had to watch from the sidelines. Cruising on those beautiful ships is like entering a whole new world where relaxation and fun times are the mode of conduct. It's an escape from the mundane cares of everyday life. "You don't even have to think on a cruise," Vincent said. The cruising industry knows how to put you in a flow that takes you where you need to be and everywhere you turn, there's always something to do so there was no space left for boredom. When my husband got into vacation mode, he had a spirit and an energy about him that left no room for boredom. "Lo, let's do this or let's go here," he would say, and I was always ready to do what he wanted just as he was ready to do what I wanted.

Our dinner reservation was for the earlier time, and we requested a table that sat four guests, us and two others. The couple that sat with us were newlyweds and they were on the cruise for their honeymoon, so the atmosphere was set to have great evenings full of enjoyable conversation at dinner because we loved being married and loved talking about marriage with others. There was an elderly gentleman who sat at a table near us at dinner, and about three days into the cruise, he walked up to my husband and asked how long we had been married. "We are celebrating fifteen years," Vincent responded.

"I admire your marriage," the gentleman said. When he said that, it took Vincent and I totally by surprise because we had not had any interaction with the gentleman.

"Thank you," we said and just looked at each other with bewildered faces, not understanding why he made that comment. We often got comments like that from those who knew us and had spent time with us, but never from a total stranger. Was it something we did or something we said that gave him that impression of us? I mean, we had not said anything to this gentleman; maybe given him a head nod to acknowledge him. We couldn't make sense of his comment because we were just being ourselves. Still, the comment meant a lot to us, and we were grateful that God had given us the marriage we had that even a stranger could not deny that it was something special.

Our first port of call was Grand Turk in the Turks and Caicos Islands and our tour guide took us through the town and showed us the business part such as the post office and supermarket. As we went further, we saw neighborhoods with homes and donkeys everywhere. The donkeys were lying in the streets like stray dogs, which was shockingly strange because I had never seen that back in the states. We came upon a small lake that had dried up and the bottom of it was white, so we asked the tour guide what caused it to be that color. He informed us that it was a saltwater lake and the white salt was left at the bottom.

Our first stop on the tour was a small cafe, which was also a juke joint. The natives were outside playing live music and dancing while others were inside getting a bite to eat. They were having a good time and some of the passengers from the cruise ship joined in with the dancing. If my leg had not been injured, we probably would have been dancing too; but it was enjoyable to watch the others dancing and enjoying the music. Our next stop was the beach and it was one of the most serene beaches I had ever been to. As we pulled up in the van, it looked like a park with trees and grass. We parked in the grass and walked down to the shore. The beach was not crowded with people and the combination of the breeze, the clear blue sky, and the sun's rays glistening down on us made the perfect recipe for relaxation. We could have stayed there all day but we had to leave with our driver. After taking a couple of pictures and recorded footage, we returned to leave with our tour guide who took us back to the ship.

"Lo, I want to go back to the cafe and get some conch fritters," Vincent said. I was down with going where there was music and dancing. When we returned to the ship, we ate lunch and relaxed for a little while. Then later, we went back to the café and Vincent got his conch fritters. I did not eat anything at the cafe because I don't eat off the ship when I cruise, but I enjoyed being there with Vincent as he enjoyed his conch fritters.

As we were walking back to the ship after the tour driver dropped us off, Vincent was recording the scenery and he asked me to say something to the camera. As I was talking, two older women were returning to the ship as well and one of them stopped, looked into the camera, and said, "She's a lovely lady."

"I agree with you," Vincent responded with a big grin on his face.

The next stop was San Juan, Puerto Rico, and while there, we went hiking through a rain forest. We had to take a 30-minute bus trip to the rain forest, then a 45-minute hike up a trail to arrive at a waterfall. I was limping the entire trail but we still enjoyed our time together. The trail was full of trees and brush and as I walked along, I said, "Lions, and tigers, and bears, oh my," like Dorothy and her friends did in the Wizard of Oz. That is how dense the forest was and there was also a mist because of the elevation we were at.

Vincent made sure I walked in front of him on the trail to keep me in his sight because my leg was still painful.

"Lo, you alright?" he asked several times as we made our way up the trail.

"Yea, bae, I'm fine," I answered. Several of the hikers stopped, taking short breaks because of exhaustion, and some turned back and did not finish the trail at all. It was an exciting time for me, so I limped on. Finally, we made it to the waterfall and it was well worth the hike to see this beautiful scene in the middle of the rainforest. It was like the pot of gold at the end of the rainbow. What an adventure it was because neither one of us had ever done anything like that in our lives. Then we quickly realized that just as we had hiked 45 minutes to reach the waterfall, we had to hike another 45 minutes to get back to where we started from. Vincent had the video recorder getting our expedition on film because he enjoyed recording our vacations and showing the footage to family and friends.

Our next port of call was St. Thomas, U.S. Virgin Islands, and we had to board a smaller boat to get to the island. We had to go up three lengthy steps to get out of the boat, which aggravated my leg injury. Even with the increased pain, we continued with a tour of the island but we cut it short. While touring a rum-making factory, we took several pictures and Vincent sampled the rum. We also went into several shops and did some shopping before returning to the ship. On the cruise line's private islands, Vincent did a jet ski excursion while I watched from the shore.

Although we had been on several cruises before, we both agreed that one was the best we had ever been on because it was just us alone, doing us; not having to consider others for seven days. When we returned home, a married person from our church asked us, "Y'all came back friends after being on the cruise together for that long?" which was a strange question to me coming from a person who had years of marriage under his belt.

Our answer was, "Yes." Then I went on to say, "Why shouldn't we still be friends? We were friends before we went on the cruise."

Chapter 10

About That Summer

The summer of 2011 proved to be a season of eventful, memorable times for us. Victor and his daughter Sibel came to visit us for two months from Turkey. When Vincent knew Victor's time of arrival to the states was approaching, he got the excitement bug and the planning began. It was all about "When Victor gets here, we're going here and we're going there." Initially, I was jealous of Victor because when he would come to visit, he got too much of Vincent's attention and it was a bit of an annoyance for me. However, as time went on I learned that was just that twin connection they had and I embraced it. Afterall, he was only here for a visit. Months ahead of their arrival, the vacation itinerary was planned with our destinations and hotel reservations.

About a month before Victor arrived that year, I fell and broke my elbow. My husband and I went to a funeral and while walking through the parking lot going up to the church, he walked ahead of me. Then I heard him say, "Lo, watch your step."

"Okay," I said as I continued walking while looking at my cell phone to turn it off so that it wouldn't ring in the church. I could see Vincent out of the corner of my eye and he kept walking, so I didn't think there was anything I had to step over because I didn't see him alter his walking or step over anything. Then I tripped over something and as hard as I tried, I could not regain my footing; I hit the ground and I hit it hard.

"Girl, I told you to watch your step," Vincent said scolding me for not listening to him while he helped me up. Embarrassed, I jumped up as fast as I could, hoping that no one had seen me fall but a couple of the church ushers saw me and came over to make sure I was not hurt. I had tripped over a concrete parking stop and my right knee and left elbow were skinned up badly. After Vincent helped me up, we went inside the church and I headed straight to the restroom to try and get myself together. I went inside one of the stalls to use it and while pulling my underwear up, I noticed a sharp pain in my right arm. Then I realized that I could barely move it. As we were walking into the church, I saw several friends whom I had not seen in a long time and as I reached to greet and embrace them, I noticed the sharp pain again and it prevented me from giving a full embrace.

"Vincent, let's sit in the back of the church in case we have to leave early," I said because I was not feeling well. After sitting for about ten minutes, I started feeling lightheaded. "Vincent, I'm not feeling good," I said.

"You ready to go?" he asked.

"Yeah," I answered, and we walked out of the church. As we walked through the parking lot to the car, I started feeling faint but I didn't say anything to Vincent until we were in the car. "I feel like I'm bout to faint bae; we have to get to the hospital."

"Where is the hospital?" Vincent asked because we were in a city that he was not familiar with. I knew the city since I used to live in it, so I tried to direct him to the hospital. Barely able to see or hear, my sense of direction was null and void.

"I am going out on you, bae," I said because I could feel myself losing consciousness. "Turn the air up; I need air," I said as I laid my head back on the headrest. Vincent turned the air on high and I was taking deep breaths as that seemed to help. He was trying to find the hospital but was unsuccessful. After about what seemed to be two or three minutes to me, but it was more like ten minutes, I said, "I believe I can make it to Sanford's hospital," because I began to feel somewhat better. Thankfully, I was sitting in the car because if I had been standing, I would have collapsed to the ground. We made it to the hospital in Sanford and discovered that I had broken my right elbow in the fall.

Vincent called the children to inform them that I had broken my elbow. After we returned home from the hospital, they all came to the house to see how I was doing. My elbow felt fine, but because of the pain medicine I took at the hospital, I was not feeling well at all. I was nauseous and each time I tried to lift my head, the room started spinning so I tried not to move much. I believe it would have been better for me to feel the pain in my elbow than the misery I felt from taking the pain pill. When our children and grandchildren came to the house, Vincent decided to reenact my fall; I couldn't help but laugh as I tried to lift my head to watch.

"Me and your mother were walking up to the church. I saw the parking stop, so I told her to watch her step and she said okay. Next thing I know, she was on the ground and all I could see was hair," he said because I wore a curly wig. Then he put my wig on, walked a couple of steps, pretended to trip over something, fell, and lay on the floor with his face toward the ground to show how I was laid out and what the hair looked like.

As I watched him on the floor, I thought to myself, "He's right, that is a lot of hair."

Vincent went on to say, "When I saw her laying on the ground, I was wondering what she was doing down there," and we all laughed. He took what was a serious situation and turned it into hilarious entertainment for us all.

The following morning when I woke up, I was so thankful that I felt better and I said to Vincent, "What a difference a day makes," and I began singing "A New Day Has Come" by Celine Dion. I did not feel any pain in my elbow and more importantly, I did not feel the misery I felt the night before from the pain medication.

My birthday is June 30th and Victor's arrival in the states for his summer vacation was usually a week or two before that. That summer it was no different, only that year I was turning "50". It is a tradition in our family to celebrate that milestone with all our siblings by planning a big party and the birthday person has no participation in the planning. Instead of my siblings doing all the planning, Vincent wanted to have his say in the planning as well. "Girl, you so nosy," Vincent often said of me because if he's doing something or going somewhere, I want to know the what's and the why's. He said he found it hard to get anything past me. After my birthday party when I found out he was having secret meetings with my sisters, I was surprised and wondered how I had no knowledge of it.

My husband rented a venue to have my party, which was different from the previous siblings' 50th birthday parties that we held at one of our homes. He and our kids hired a DJ and had some of the food catered. My sisters oversaw the decorations, and the food that the caterer did not supply was prepared by my family; my nieces were the servers. Vincent kept me so out of the loop with my party that one day as Victor was taking a cooler from our home, he noticed me looking at him with a puzzled look on my face. Without me asking him anything, he said, "Oh, we need the cooler because we are having a get-together at Mom's."

"Oh, okay," I said. But I thought to myself, "Vincent didn't tell me anything about a get-together." After the party, we were all sitting around talking and Victor informed me that he needed the cooler for my party but he couldn't tell me that, so he had to quickly come up with another reason why he needed it; we all laughed.

As we arrived at the venue, Vincent escorted me in. I was delighted to see my family and friends that came to celebrate with me. Vincent had my best friend Geralyn and her husband Robert seated at the table with us along with my mom and his mom. To my surprise, Vincent contacted my friend Eddie, who lives in another state, and he came to my party as well. There were also several friends there from the church we attended. Vincent, along with my kids, put together a program and Victor was the emcee. One by one, my family members and a few friends spoke about me. Our grandbabies were the only kids Vincent allowed at the party because he knew I would want them to be there; they made their grand entrance as 'The "Three Divas.'"

After eating my birthday dinner, with my arm still in a brace from the fall, Vincent and I danced the rest of the evening. In fact, I don't think we sat at all once we started dancing. We were known for dancing and we really enjoyed dancing with each other. "If I ever have a party, I want y'all to be there because y'all know how to get the party started," my brother Dennis said to me. When we attended a party, guests who knew us expected us to be on the dance floor and we did not disappoint. We danced to every song the DJ played that evening.

It was a great celebration with my family and friends. After the party, my sister Gail said, "Girl, your husband had you. He let us know what he did and did not want for your party. He knew how he wanted your party to go and he let anyone who had other ideas know how it was gon go."

Vincent's itinerary for our summer vacation included a road trip for the month of July and a cruise for the month of August. Me, Vincent, Victor, Vincent Jr., and Sibel went on the road trip together. Our first stop was in Savannah, Georgia. and while there, we did a bus tour to the first schoolhouse, an old graveyard, a hanging tree, the first African American church and several other sites. We also did one of the boat tours and because I was such a fan of Paula Deen's cooking show, we ate at her restaurant. The hotel we stayed at was within walking distance of the pier, downtown, and the restaurants; we enjoyed walking to the different spots and talking together as we went. We did not move our car until we checked out of the hotel.

Our next stop was Atlanta. and Vincent had a friend who lived there whose name also was Victor. Of course, he wanted Victor his brother to meet Victor his friend. Billy, another good friend of Vincent's also lived in Atlanta, so he informed both his friends that we were coming. When Victor the friend heard we were coming to Atlanta, he began planning for our visit and was able to get us free tickets to the Atlanta Aquarium, the Coco-Cola factory, and the HLN Newsroom. On the last day of our stay in Atlanta, Billy met us around noon at the mall that was close to the hotel where we were staying, and Vincent and his brother spent that evening with him. The following morning, we went to Vincent's nephew Antione's house who also lived in Atlanta and spent the day and the night with him and his family. Then rising early, we headed for Chattanooga, Tennessee. We spent two days there and went to the caves at Ruby Falls and Look Out Mountain before returning home.

For his mom's birthday earlier that year in February, Vincent gave her a card that said his and Victor's gift that year was a cruise planned for the summer. She was happy because she enjoys traveling and spending time with her children. It was Vincent and Victor's hope that their siblings would join us on the cruise and some said they were going. However, when Vincent began planning and paying for the cruise, none of the other siblings showed interest in going. So, it was just me, Vincent, Victor, Vincent Jr., Fantasy, Sibel and Mom who went on the cruise. Vincent and Victor were disappointed because they were always trying to get the family together.

We did a five-day cruise to the Bahamas; Cozumel, Mexico; and Key West, Florida. Vincent took his video recorder to get footage so that we could have memories of the time we spent together. As I reminisce, I am so glad we have the recordings although Vincent was not recorded much because he was the one who usually did the recording, but we can hear his voice. On the final evening of the cruise, we went out on deck and did a final recording of us saying how much we enjoyed the cruise and being with each other and everyone had to say something. "Come join us will ya," Vincent said because he wanted to encourage his other siblings to join us on the next family cruise not knowing that was the last family cruise he would take.

The summer of 2011 also proved to be a time of awakening for us. After celebrating our fifteenth-year wedding anniversary the previous year and having one of the most celebrated summers I can remember with family and friends, Vincent was diagnosed with cancer. I'm not going to call it a rude awakening, but it was definitely not in accordance with the summer we were having.

Victor and Sibel had returned to Turkey in the earlier part of August of that year, and we were just getting back into some normalcy when Vincent walked through the door of our apartment after a workout at the gym in our complex. His shirt was spotted with proof of a sweaty workout with wet spots in the front and in the back. He stopped in the kitchen where I was preparing dinner and he asked, "Lo, you'll get me some water?" I gave him a glass of water and after drinking it, he headed to the bathroom to take a shower. Shortly thereafter, I heard him say, "Lo, come here," so I went to the bathroom to see what he wanted. As I turned the corner to enter the bathroom, I saw Vincent standing in the mirror, shirtless with both arms flexed. "You see this knot under my arm?" he asked. Vincent had a nice pair of arms and when he flexed them, his biceps raised up like two large grapefruits. He was not a big muscular man, but he worked out and kept himself in shape.

Looking at the golf ball-sized knot sitting in the pit of his left arm, I said, "Yeah, I see it."

"What is it?" Vincent asked, looking at me as if I could answer the question. I had no idea what it was but I knew it should not have been there.

"I don't know what that is. Does it bother you?" I asked.

With his left arm lifted, he answered, "No, I just notice when I lift weights, this arm gets tired before the other one does." Shrugging his shoulders while continuing to undress, he said, "I don't know what it is either, but I'll call to make an appointment to the doctor." Oddly enough, we did not discuss the knot again until after he went to see the doctor, which was about a week or so later. The reason for that may have been because the knot did not cause him any pain or bothersome discomfort, so I did not think it was anything to be concerned about.

Notably, Vincent was in great health. If there was a picture of health, he would have been it. He did not miss his annual physicals and he didn't have any health issues or concerns. Vincent didn't have any problems with his blood pressure, his cholesterol levels were always good, and he never had a problem with his weight. Also, because cancer was in his family's medical history, he had yearly prostate exams beginning at the age of forty; and for extra precaution, he had a colonoscopy at the age of forty-three. His father and most of his paternal aunts and uncles had cancer, so he took the extra precautionary measures of early cancer examinations. His doctor thought the growth might have been the result of an infection. He prescribed an antibiotic and told him to take it for ten days. I thought to myself, "Surely, that must be what it is; he will take the antibiotics as directed and after the ten days the growth will be gone."

After completing the antibiotics treatment, the growth was still as prominent as before. Vincent made another appointment with the doctor for further instructions. His doctor advised him to make an appointment at a surgery center to have the growth surgically removed and Vincent did as the doctor recommended. On the morning of the scheduled surgery, we arrived at the surgery center and after checking in, the doctor came out and told us how long the surgery would last. I don't recall how long he said the surgery would last, but I do remember waiting longer than expected. When the doctor finally came out to the waiting area, it seemed to me that he was coming to speak with another family that was waiting and seeing me was a happenstance that reminded him that I was waiting for word on Vincent's surgery.

Turning his attention toward me he said, "I don't know what that was. I couldn't get it all because it was all wrapped up in some nerves in his arm and I didn't want to damage the nerves, so I got what I could. We'll send it off to see what it is. He's in recovery now and you can go back with him." The doctor also informed me that Vincent would have a drain line for a couple of days and that we needed to call his office for a follow-up appointment.

"Okay, thank you," was my response to the doctor as he proceeded to walk over and speak with someone else who was waiting. Although I thought it was odd that the doctor had me waiting much longer than he initially told me, I still didn't think much of what he said. But I had a picture in my mind of the remaining lump as an exposed pink fleshly vulnerable wound in my husband's arm pit and that could not be good for him.

When I went back to the recovery room, Vincent was still drowsy from the anesthesia. We had to wait for about another hour in recovery before they discharged him to go home. While we waited, I told Vincent what the doctor said and his response was, "Okay."

Also, we had some entertainment from another patient in the recovery room: "Hey, can I have some more of that?" we heard in slurred speech coming from one of the recovery pods. After a short pause, we heard it again, "Hey, can I have some more of that?" Vincent and I started laughing and the nurse came in and saw us laughing and said, "There's a young high school student requesting to have some more of the meds he was given for the anesthesia; it's the same medicine Michael Jackson's doctor administered to him."

"Well, that must be some good stuff," Vincent said, and we both laughed.

Vincent called the doctor's office to make an appointment for a follow-up visit, and he asked the nurse if she could tell him the results from the tests of the growth in his arm pit over the phone. She told him he would have to speak to the doctor about the results. Vincent's follow-up appointment to the surgery was scheduled for October 20th, his 46th birthday, and we both went to the appointment. The doctor came into the room where we were waiting and informed us that the tumor was malignant. Also, he said it was an aggressive type of cancer and recommended that Vincent see a cancer doctor. He went on to say, "Not just one from around here, but a cancer center such as MD Anderson in Orlando or Moffit in Tampa."

I don't know how to explain my reaction, but it wasn't the normal unsettling reaction that I heard others had when receiving the same news. And as for Vincent, he didn't give any indication of fear or distraught. He just said, "Okay." When the doctor left the room, Vincent looked at me and said, "I knew it was cancer when the nurse told me I would have to talk to the doctor about the results." I know that it would make for better reading if there had been more drama and crying after receiving the diagnosis of cancer from the doctor, but we were surprisingly calm.

I didn't know what to say to Vincent but "You're special" came to mind so I said it, and Vincent looked at me with a perplexed expression. "God chose you for this," I said.

During the ride home, we discussed telling our children of the news we had just received and since it was his birthday, we knew that they were coming to the house. Our oldest son Delrick and his wife Tamika came over with their daughters, Lauryn, Morgan, and Aniston. Our daughter Fantasy also came over; and our youngest son Vincent Jr. still lived with us, so he was there too. Vincent called the kids together in the living room to give them the news. "Well, the tests came back from the growth and it's cancer," he said. He went on to tell them what the doctor advised about going to a cancer center because of the type of cancer it was. The countenance on their faces changed because they came to celebrate his birthday, but the news of the cancer overshadowed the celebration. Seeing the concern on their faces, Vincent quickly changed the mood in the room and said, "But we are going to trust God and I will be alright," as he clasped his hands in finality. With a smile on his face, he continued, "Today is my birthday and me and your mother bout to go out to dinner to celebrate; y'all don't worry about nothing cause God's got this." My daughter-in-law said it was so weird to her because Vincent and I did not seem troubled at all by the news of the cancer. Although the diagnosis seemed unfavorable, Vincent communicated it and encouraged them with the hope that he had.

For Vincent's birthday celebration, we had dinner at Fish Bones, which was one of his favorite restaurants. Vincent usually ordered the medium-well ribeye steak or the grilled pork chops and that evening, steak was his choice. "Umm, umm, boy this steak is slammin!" he said as he finished his first bite. I enjoyed seeing and hearing him enjoy his food because if it was good, he let it be known. The cancer diagnosis did not consume our conversation that evening. Instead, we enjoyed a great dinner along with a glass of wine with which I toasted him and looked forward to celebrating many more birthdays together. Then we left the restaurant and finished his birthday celebration at home in our bedroom.

Receiving the diagnosis of cancer did not alter Vincent's attitude about enjoying life. Along with preparing for Victor and Sibel's arrival that summer, Vincent and I were also planning a married couples cruise for our church. The married couples cruise was set to sail approximately three weeks after we received the cancer diagnosis. Our pastor and his wife were the only ones we informed because we did not want anyone to be overly concerned and diminish our excitement about going on the cruise or dampen the mood of the nineteen other married couples joining us. We kept the news to a select few people. We wanted everyone to enjoy the cruise and that is what we did.

The cruise was set to sail in November of that same year. The ship left the port on a Monday and returned the following Friday. On the first night of the cruise, Vincent and I went back to our cabin after dinner so that I could change clothes to go dancing later. Vincent put the key in the door to open our cabin and to my surprise as I stepped into the room, rose petals adorned the bed and a bottle of wine was in a bucket chilling on ice. He took pleasure in my happiness from the special ways he showed his love for me.

One year for our anniversary (when I was working third shift), he came to my job and filled my car with balloons while I was inside working. I had left the house to arrive at work at 11pm. When I walked out to my car the following morning to leave my job, the closer I got to my car, I thought, "That's not my car," because it was filled with balloons and that was not the way I left it. Then I took a second look and thought, "Wait, that is my car." Vincent had filled the car with "I Love You" and "Happy Anniversary" balloons. As soon as I got in the car, I began dialing the phone for home. Vincent said he was counting down the seconds because he knew I would be calling him. "Vincent!" I shrieked when he answered the phone.

He started laughing and said, "Gotcha."

"When did you do that?" I asked. He told me he waited about thirty minutes after I left, called the guard shack on my job, got permission to come out there, and came and put the balloons in my car.

"I just wish I could've been there to see your reaction," he said. So when I walked in the cabin on the cruise and saw what he had done,

I looked at him smiling and he was looking at me with that big *gotcha* grin on his face.

"How did you do this? When did you set this up?" I asked. While looking at the rose petals and the wine, I couldn't help but wonder how he found the time to set the surprise up on the cruise ship because I had been with him the entire time.

"I called the cruise line and set it up," he said still grinning. Then he asked, "Well, you ready to change clothes and go back out?"

After I walked into our cabin and saw the surprise he had for me, I said, "Oh, we are not going anywhere." Vincent closed the door and we rolled around in those rose petals for a while. Then we had a glass of wine before going out to join the other couples.

Chapter 11

No Need to Panic

If Vincent did not inform others that he had cancer, then it would not have been known because he continued with his life as usual. He told his mom and his family about the diagnosis, but he also let them know that he was trusting God in the situation and he wanted them to trust God too. I didn't say anything to anyone because I knew cancer was nothing for God to heal, so I was not really concerned about it. It was not anything to make much ado about, and I didn't want others to either. My thoughts were, "God is going to use this to show us more of Him and this is just something we have to go through." We had previously gone through an illness with our daughter Fantasy, and we did not know if she was going to survive it. But it was in that ordeal with Fantasy that God revealed Himself to us like never before. We knew that God uses what we might deem as unfavorable situations to bring more clarity of Him, so we were not in despair.

About five years before Vincent's cancer diagnosis, Fantasy had taken deathly ill. Early one morning before daylight, I was wakened by Fantasy calling, "Ma."

Coming out of a deep sleep, I answered, "Huh?"

"Come here," she said. I reluctantly got up out of bed and went into the living room to see her reeling in pain on the floor.

"My stomach hurts bad," she said.

"Did you take anything for the pain?" I asked.

"Yes, but it still hurts," she said.

"Just give the medicine time to work," I said because I just wanted to go back to bed.

"Ma, it hurts really bad; I believe I need to go the hospital," she said.

"Just give it a few minutes to see if you feel better," I said because the hospital was the last place I wanted to be. It was about 4am and I wanted my bed, not the bright lights and coldness of a hospital emergency room. "Vincent," I said as I walked back to our bedroom, "Fantasy's stomach hurts and she wants to go to the hospital."

"What?" he said trying to wake up. I repeated what I had just said while lying back in my bed hoping her stomach pains would subside but they got worse.

"Ma," she called again, "I need to go to the hospital."

"You sure?" I asked because Fantasy can be a bit of an exaggerator when it comes to pain.

"Yes," she said.

Vincent and I got up out of bed, got dressed and took Fantasy to the emergency room. After examining her and taking x-rays, the ER doctor told us they had to airlift Fantasy to Shands Hospital in Gainesville. He went on to say that she had a blood clot in her portal vein that was preventing blood flow to her intestines and liver, and he was afraid that a portion of her intestines was dead and her liver could be damaged. "We're not equipped here at this hospital to deal with this illness, so I have arranged for her to be transported to Shands," the doctor said. While Fantasy was enroute to Shands by helicopter, Vincent and I went home, grabbed some clothes and toiletries, and drove two hours to arrive at Shands Hospital. Not understanding the seriousness of Fantasy's illness and thinking that she would have surgery and be out of the hospital in two or three days, we only grabbed enough clothes for a couple of days. Little did we know that a couple of days would turn into seven weeks.

By the time we arrived at Shands, Fantasy was already in surgery and the receptionist in the waiting area advised us that the doctor would come to speak with us there. After the surgery, a doctor came to the waiting area to inform us that Fantasy was out of surgery and was in recovery. He went on to say that they had to check her liver and every inch of her intestines to make sure that no part of her intestines was dead because of the restricted blood flow caused by the blood clot. After discovering that there was no damage, the doctor said they had started Fantasy on a heparin drip (which is a blood thinner) because the blood clot was still there. Since the surgery went well and the blood clot did not cause any damage, Vincent and I were thankful and believed this ordeal would be over soon. We did not know there were other medical problems looming.

Fantasy's surgery was invasive; that's the word the surgeon used. He had to cut her from her sternum to the top of her pubic area to check for damage to her organs. In addition, because the infamous blood clot was still there and the doctors were giving her a blood thinner, Fantasy had excessive bleeding in her stomach. The doctors had to take her back into surgery because her stomach swelled due to the excessive bleeding. The hematologist and the head trauma surgeon were in a complicated situation as to what was the best treatment. The hematologist wanted to keep her on a blood thinner because of the blood clot and the head trauma surgeon knew that the blood thinner was contributing to the excessive bleeding. Although blood thinner and surgery do not make for good bed-fellows, the doctors continued the blood thinner because the blood clot remained, and her intestines and liver were still in danger of losing blood flow.

One day as Vincent and I were walking into Fantasy's hospital room, we noticed a group of doctors standing outside of her room having a conversation, but we did not know that it was about her. As we entered the room, Fantasy asked, "Did y'all talk to the doctors?"

"No," we responded.

"I think y'all need to talk to them," she said. After talking with the doctors, we learned that they were bringing in a specialist from Miami whom they hoped could perform a procedure to get rid of the blood clot.

When the specialist came, he was surprised to see the size of the blood clot, which he compared to a ten-dollar quarter roll. He said it was one of the largest he had ever seen. Also, he explained to us the scope of the procedure he planned to do: "We will have to go through the carotid artery in her neck guiding a needle down to the blood clot and dropping the meds directly on the clot in hopes of dissolving it. This is a very dangerous procedure because the path of the needle will be very close to her lungs and there is the possibility that the lungs can be punctured." We all agreed along with Fantasy to have the procedure done, so they scheduled it for the next morning.

After the first day's procedure, the doctor sent Fantasy to ICU and placed her in an induced coma. The specialist performed the procedure for three consecutive days to have the meds dropped directly on the clot to dissolve it but to no avail. It became so disheartening and overwhelming to walk in that ICU room day after day for those three days and watch our daughter in an induced coma, bleeding like a slaughtered pig from that hole in the carotid artery in her neck, which remained open for the duration of the procedure. Although we knew about the risks of the procedure, we did not expect Fantasy to be unresponsive or to see blood dripping from her neck. The doctors did not disclose that part of the procedure to us and it was difficult for me and Vincent to endure.

The nurses kept her neck wrapped in a towel which I am sure was white when they initially wrapped it around her neck; but by the time we arrived at the hospital, the towel was red, soaked with her blood.

When the doctors saw that the procedure did nothing to dissolve the clot, they closed the hole in her neck and Fantasy's condition went downhill from there. She remained in the induced coma and her whole body began to swell. We might not have understood the seriousness of her illness initially, but it was certainly becoming clear to us. To see Fantasy hooked up to a breathing machine, looking like a blow-up Pillsbury Dough Boy balloon in a parade was very unsettling for me. She was retaining so much fluid that when the nurses took cultures to check for infections, the fluid seeped out of the holes left by the needles and soaked her bed sheets.

One day, the head trauma surgeon called my husband and I into the consultation room and with tears in his eyes, he said, "We're losing the battle. If we don't operate on Fantasy, her organs will start shutting down because she's retaining too much fluid. On the other hand, if we do operate, she could bleed to death and die. What do you all want us to do? You make the decision."

Through my tears, I said, "You can't just let my baby die."

"So you want us to operate?" he asked.

"Yes," Vincent and I both said.

"Alright, we will operate." Fantasy's condition was so critical that the doctor said he did not think she would make it to the operating room, so they transformed the ICU into an operating room. The nurses who worked in the ICU said they had never seen it done before. Fantasy survived the surgery, but her condition was still critical. Instead of closing her stomach with staples, which is what was done after the first surgery, the surgeon applied a wound vac so the blood could drain and the wound could heal from the inside out.

My understanding of faith at that time was that if we believed God and not doubt, that God would perform what we were believing him to do. But I had never been in a life and death situation. I didn't know whether Fantasy was going to live or die. I asked my husband, "Vincent, if Fantasy dies, does it mean we don't have faith?"

"No, Lo, that don't mean we don't have faith, but that could be our reality. God is in control," he said. I agreed with him, but the question about faith still lingered on my mind.

The next morning in prayer, I began to question God about faith because I wanted understanding: "Now Lord, I have seen families who don't seem to have you on their mind and their loved ones get sick and you raise their loved ones up and they live. Then I have seen families whose loved ones get sick and they worship you and love you, and yet their loved ones die. So Lord, who am I and what difference does it make that I worship and love you? How much do I have to pray for you to raise Fantasy up?" I wondered if my relationship with God even mattered as to whether she would live or die. Surprisingly, the Lord answered me; that does not happen often.

I wanted a response but I was not expecting one. However, He clearly spoke to me and said, "It's not what you do, it's what I've done."

When God answered, it startled me and I stopped praying at that moment because I did not know what else to say. God had spoken and the words He spoke were all I needed to hear. His words lifted a weight off of me I had been carrying because I thought it was all on me: that if I had faith, prayed and believed, Fantasy would not die. We all hear it in church and from the 'religious' people, "Just have faith," or "If you believe God will do it, He will do it." Or better yet, "If He did it for me, He will do it for you." So then if she dies, does that mean I had not prayed and believed hard enough? And does that mean I don't have enough faith?

When my family and friends called to encourage me, some would say 'Just have faith.' Well, I got so tired of hearing that and I told my husband, "If one more person says that to me, I'm gonna scream." That's what I felt like doing, but I didn't do it. I also wanted to respond and say, "What, you don't think I have faith? You don't think I believe God?" I know they were only trying to encourage me but instead, it annoyed me. That's what man's religion teaches, so I believed that whether Fantasy would live or die was dependent on what I did, but God let me know it was dependent on what He had already done. We needed encouragement, not religious cliches.

In fact, earlier that year before Fantasy's sickness, an acquaintance of ours was going through something similar with her daughter and I said the same thing they were saying to me, "Just have faith," which is the religious thing to say. After going through the ordeal with Fantasy, I was compelled to call her and ask her to forgive me for being so insensitive. It was easy for me to tell her to have faith, but when I had to walk in those shoes and heard the same thing from family and friends, I realized that telling her to 'Just have faith,' was callous and ignorant of me even though my intent was to encourage her. I was not sure if she felt as I did, but I still had to ask her for forgiveness.

After the Lord answered me, I still did not know whether Fantasy was going to live or die, but the peace I had about what we were going through was indescribably overwhelming. I shared with my husband what the Lord had said to me and my understanding: we don't have faith for God to do what we want Him to do, but we have faith for God to do what He has already done. The works of God are finished so we can pray all night and day for God to do something we want Him to do; but if it's not in His finished works, it will not happen. After God spoke to me, from that time on, it did not matter what the doctors or nurses said because I knew Fantasy's outcome was not according to what they could or could not do; it was according to the finished works of God. I didn't fully understand what that meant, but I knew the only one who knew the finished works of God was God; and the only way we can have the finished works of God is by praying in the Holy Spirit so that's what I did. Also, we were able to encourage other families with loved ones who were in ICU along with Fantasy because they saw the unshakable peace we had even though our daughter was in a dire situation. I am thankful that Fantasy is alive and doing well today but I know it is not because of anything I did; it is because of what God had already done.

When Fantasy returned to the hospital for her follow up visits, her presence was noised over the hospital and the nurses and doctors who treated her came to see her. It sounded like a celebrity had come to the hospital. We heard them saying, "Fantasy's here, Fantasy's here," as we walked down the corridor. Big smiles were on faces and each one talked about their experience of treating her.

To my surprise, the hematologist, a big and tall man (whom I called The Preacher Doctor) walked in the room with a boisterous voice that was comparable to his stature and he was praising God: "This is the day that the Lord has made, and we will rejoice and be glad in it. Your name should have been Faith instead of Fantasy because that is why you're still here. You were shot at twice and the bullet missed both times. With the clot you had, your intestines should have been dead and your liver should have been gone. But somehow, the blood found a way to get to the organs and they were not damaged at all." His expression of what he knew God had done was music to my ears. I was thankful to know that he knew Fantasy's recovery was not because of what he had done, but it was because of what God had done. It was a trying time for us all, but the glory God revealed and the peace it brought to our hearts was worth it.

After going through that experience with Fantasy, I knew that there was no sickness that God could not heal. We were thankful for the doctors, but we knew their word was not the final word; God's word was and still is the final word. Despite how dire Vincent's cancer diagnosis was, this to me was just another trial that God would use to show us even more of Him and bring more understanding of Himself just like He did with Fantasy's ordeal. I witnessed that when the doctors were at their wits end and did not know what to do for her, it was God who healed her and brought her through the sickness. Therefore, my reaction was not panic or distraught when we received the cancer diagnosis, but of calm and peace. I knew that it is what God says that determines what will be and that cancer was nothing for God to heal. I also never thought God would allow the cancer to be the end of us.

Chapter 12

Plan of Attack

Following the advice of the surgeon, Vincent made an appointment at the MD Anderson Cancer Center in Orlando. He was set up with one of the oncologists whom I will refer to as Dr. Anderson. I believe he might have been a little younger than Vincent and he was very pleasant to talk to. At the initial appointment, he not only talked about the cancer diagnosis but he also talked about his family and that he and his wife enjoyed cruises too. In subsequent visits, he talked about his enjoyment of playing basketball, which was Vincent's favorite sport activity. Dr. Anderson's conversations made the appointments personable and pleasurable. Because he and my husband had common interests, the appointments seemed as if we were going to see one of my husband's friends. They even went as far as to set up a time that they would meet at a sports complex to play basketball together. Vincent was excited about the possibility of playing basketball with Dr. Anderson, but they could never coordinate the times for them to meet.

Dr. Anderson informed us of the strategy to attack the cancer. He wanted Vincent to have the remainder of the tumor removed first. Also, he informed us that the tumor was located on the brachial plexus, which is the network of nerves that gives the arm its movement. Dr. Anderson was not a surgeon, but he did tell us that the location of the tumor complicated its removal because any damage to the nerves in that arm could cause Vincent to lose some or all the movement in that arm. The course of treatment was for Vincent to see a microsurgeon to have the remainder of the tumor removed. He referred Vincent to one in Orlando that he considered to be one of the best in the area.

I cannot recall the microsurgeon's name because we only saw him once. After looking at the results of Vincent's x-rays, the microsurgeon came into the room and asked, "Did you all see where the tumor is?" with a look of disbelief on his face.

"No," we answered. Dr. Anderson had informed us where the tumor was, but we did not understand the severity of the location of it until we saw and heard the microsurgeon's response.

"I will not do the operation because I will not be responsible for you losing the movement in your left arm. There is no way you can get that tumor without damaging those nerves," he said. For me, his response brought the gravity of the location of the tumor front and center because our focus was the cancer and not the location of it. It was eye-opening for us as to the meticulous care that the doctor had to give in removing the remainder of the tumor or if it could even be done.

"Well, if he is supposed to be one of the best microsurgeons in the area and he said he will not touch the tumor, where can we go?" I asked Vincent.

"We'll just have to let Dr. Anderson know what he said and go from there," he calmly responded.

"Yeah, you're right," I said.

We followed up with an appointment with Dr. Anderson and expressed to him what the microsurgeon told us. The only other option he knew of was a surgeon at Shands Hospital in Gainesville (whom I will refer to as Dr. Shands). He said Dr. Shands does the type of surgery Vincent needed on a regular basis. "I'll give him a call," he said. We both hoped that Dr. Shands would see Vincent and at best, be willing to attempt to remove the remainder of the tumor. After the first microsurgeon's response, we didn't know what to expect.

Thankfully, Dr. Shands consented to see Vincent and scheduled an appointment for him to come in. When Dr. Shands walked into the examination room where we were waiting, he looked at Vincent and said, "Those are some nice guns (speaking of Vincent's arms), and we can't let anything happen to them." Then he asked, "You work out?"

"Yes," Vincent replied.

"I can tell," Dr. Shands responded.

Then Vincent asked, "What happens if the nerves are damaged?"

"If the nerves are damaged, then you will lose the use of the arm and you will have a 'dead' arm. The arm will just hang limp with no movement and in that case, it is better to amputate the arm rather than have a dead arm." Dr. Shands ordered his own MRI of the tumor and after looking at the results, he confidently said, "Oh, I'm sure I can get the tumor without damaging the nerves." His response was in total contrast to the response of the first microsurgeon we saw. His demeanor exuded total confidence and assurance that he could remove the tumor and Vincent wouldn't have to worry about losing the movement of his arm. He went on to suggest the course of action he believed would be best for Vincent after the surgery. "We will give the arm six weeks to heal and then follow up with six weeks of radiation to get rid of any other cancer cells in the area. I don't recommend the chemo because the sarcoma is so dense, it most likely will not respond to chemo. The radiation should be enough."

"Alright," Vincent said as he agreed to the course of action Dr. Shands recommended.

The surgery to remove the remaining portion of the tumor was scheduled for December 14, 2011. Vincent and I along with our kids headed to Gainesville before sunset that morning because it was a two-hour drive. He checked into the hospital and was prepped for the surgery. The biggest concern was hoping Dr. Shands would be able to get all the tumor without Vincent losing the use of his left arm.

We all waited for Dr. Shands to let us know how the surgery went. "I got it all," he said as he walked towards us smiling after the surgery.

"Good," I responded smiling at him.

"The surgery went well, and you all can see him shortly."

"Okay," I said. After we saw that he was fine, the kids headed back home while I stayed at the hospital with Vincent. Because the surgery went as expected and there were no complications in his recovery, he was able to go home after just a couple of days.

About a week later, Invacare, which was Vincent's place of employment, had their annual holiday event. He enjoyed attending their events because he said they were important for building camaraderie among the employees. Therefore, it didn't surprise me when he said, "Lo, I'm going to Invacare's Christmas party."

"Are you sure you're ready?" I asked because it was so soon after his surgery.

"Yeah, I wanna go," he said. Still bandaged up from the surgery, he went to the holiday party. I thought it was too early for him to go, but he went anyway. When he returned home, he came in smiling. "Baby, I won a Paula Deen pot set for you," he said.

"Woo hoo!" I said excitedly since I was a Paula Deen fan. With the surgery being a success and getting the new pot set, that was all the Christmas I needed.

Vincent recovered quickly from the surgery and was released by the doctor to return to work. He also scheduled the six weeks of radiation with Dr. Anderson's office. The schedule for the radiation was Monday through Friday. Vincent scheduled his appointments for early morning so that he could go to work afterwards. He had just returned to work and he did not want the radiation to interfere with his work schedule. "I'm going with you to all your radiation appointments," I said.

"Lo, you don't have to do that," he said. I knew I did not have to go, but I would not have it any other way.

Vincent woke up like clockwork every morning. He did not need an alarm because he was used to waking up early. I, on the other hand, needed a little help. Each morning he'd wake me up to go with him for radiation, which was working fine until I woke up one morning and he was gone. "He left me, he left me!" I said panicking as I picked up the phone to call him. I couldn't believe he had left me, and I called him immediately.

"Hello?," he said when he answered the phone.

"Why did you leave me? You know I wanted to go."

"Girl, you were sleeping so good with your butt all tooted up in the air, I didn't want to bother you."

"Vincent, you should've woke me up. Don't do that again; you know I want to go with you."

"Okay, I won't do it again," and he didn't.

The doctor had advised Vincent to use Aquaphor, a skin protectant, after taking the radiation treatments because the radiation was known to burn the skin. After each treatment, we went home, I rubbed his underarm area down with the Aquaphor, and Vincent went on to work. That was our routine during the radiation treatments. After the last treatment, Vincent received a certificate of completion from the radiation department and rang the bell to celebrate the completion with a big smile and great attitude. I brought my camera that morning to capture the moment. We were both happy that the early morning drives to Orlando were over.

With the tumor removed and the radiation completed, I was sure we were done with the cancer and thought that Vincent had completed the radiation without any burn to his underarm. Vincent went in to work that Saturday morning to do some maintenance at the job and he had to paint the floors. The friction from moving his arm back and forth while painting irritated the skin at the site of the radiation and the area became raw. It looked as if he had been burned under his arm. Vincent just took it all in stride and didn't let that stop him from his everyday goings and doings. I continued to rub the area with Aquaphor and it soon healed.

Thankfully, Vincent didn't have any nerve damage from the surgery, but he did develop some lymphedema in his left hand which caused it to swell. Dr. Shands said that was because he had to remove some lymph nodes as well during the surgery. He then advised Vincent to be fitted for a glove to help with the circulation and to keep the swelling to a minimum, so we found a place in our hometown and they measured his hand for the glove and ordered it for him. The glove was black with the fingers cut out and he wore it all the time except when he slept because it did help keep the swelling to a minimum. He also had to have some physical therapy to strengthen and maintain flexibility in his arm. His sister Stacy, worked at a rehabilitation center and was able to get him in for some physical therapy sessions. In the therapy sessions, they showed him how to use a resistance band and they allowed him to keep one to use after the sessions were done so he could continue his physical therapy at home.

The doctors scheduled Vincent to have an MRI in three months and then another one three months later; and if those MRIs were good, he wouldn't need another one for six months. Both doctors received copies of the first MRI and Dr. Anderson said it looked like Vincent had torn something in his shoulder. While at home, I helped Vincent with his stretching, so he said, "Girl you done tore something in my shoulder."

"I ain't tore nothing; all I did was help you with your stretching," I said. I wasn't sure if I had damaged his shoulder or not, but I didn't think the stretching was too intense. When we went back to Dr. Shands, we told him what Dr. Anderson said about a tear and he said, "No, I had to remove it, it wasn't torn." I was so thankful and relieved to hear Dr. Shands say that because I didn't want to be the cause of any more injury to Vincent's shoulder. Dr. Shands also mentioned that although he didn't think the cancer would return, if it did, then Vincent should consider the possibility of amputation to decrease the risk of the cancer spreading to his lungs. "Because of the type of cancer you have, if it spreads to the lungs, there's not much more we could do for you," he said. I heard what Dr. Shands said and I kept it in mind, but I wasn't worried because I didn't think we would ever have to cross that bridge.

Chapter 13

Cancer Free?

After the surgery and radiation, Vincent was back to his old self. He was playing basketball, playing tennis, working out, and participating in other activities he enjoyed. We were not able to go on a vacation that summer because Vincent was the only one employed at the time and with the medical bills and him having to take time off from work for the surgeries, we had to forgo vacations that year. However, for his birthday in October of that year, we went to Miami for a few days. Miami was one of our favorite getaway spots. All we needed was a few days to go to South Beach for sightseeing and the lively atmosphere, then to Coconut Grove for the relaxed atmosphere and on to Bayside to listen to live music and maybe a boat tour. Our Miami getaways were usually in April for our anniversary or during the summer months when Victor came to the states. But because we had not taken a vacation that year and we just felt like we needed to do something for his birthday and Miami was the ticket.

Being in Miami in October was unexpectedly calm and the weather was simply perfect because it was not hot and humid; we were not sweating, but it was warm enough to dress like it was still summer. Whenever we went in April, it was during spring break and as for the weather, it was the beginning of summer and South Beach was packed with partying, sweaty, half-naked people. We enjoyed watching the myriads of people enjoying themselves because we knew how to be there with them and not be a part of the scene. While visiting South Beach in October, strolling down the sidewalks on Ocean Avenue was more pleasant and we were able to walk side by side. There was no need to walk behind my husband because of the crowds walking in single file lines up one side of the sidewalk and down the other side of the sidewalk. It was apparent that October is not a popular time for young people on South Beach. There was more of a middle-aged ambiance going on, which we did not expect but it was an enjoyable surprise.

I thought South Beach was always the party place to be any time of year. When we were there during the peak times of spring break and summer, there was no time to partake in a conversation with someone passing by; but while walking down the sidewalk on Ocean Drive, a gentleman stopped my husband and asked him if he was a doctor. "No," Vincent responded, and the gentleman went on to ask him about the glove he was wearing. In fact, they talked for a few minutes; but if it had been during the summer, that would not have happened. We were both amazed at how relaxing the atmosphere was at that time of year and we agreed to make that a destination for his future birthdays.

The first MRI Vincent had was in May of 2012 and the result was that there was no cancer. That was great news for us but not surprising because we did not expect the cancer to return. The next MRI was three months later which was August of that same year and it came back clear, no cancer. The first two MRIs were done and the next MRI was due in six months, which was February of the following year. At the New Year's Eve service at our church each year, there is a time in which different ones stand and testify as to the goodness of God. That year, my husband testified and thanked God that he was cancer-free, and we all praised God with him. However, in February at the next MRI, Dr. Shands informed us that he saw a spot and believed it was cancer. They took more tests to confirm whether or not it was cancer, and it was.

What does the term 'cancer-free' really mean to the people who believed they were cancer- free only to have the cancer return later? Although "cancer-free" sounds great to say and hear especially to the one diagnosed with it, I believe "no cancer detected" is a more realistic phrase. In the previous scans, the cancer was not detected; but in my non-medical opinion, it had to have been there all the time. Dr. Shands recommended that Vincent take chemo to see if it would shrink the tumor and immediately my mind was taken back to one of our earlier visits with him in which he told us that because of the denseness of the tumor, it most likely will not respond to chemo. If that was his thought, why recommend chemo? It seemed to me that Dr. Shands was grasping for straws and hoping that the chemo would shrink the tumor so that he could avoid amputating Vincent's arm. I was hoping Vincent would never have to take chemo because I had heard of how it can adversely affect the person receiving it, but he agreed to start taking chemo and I supported him in his decision. The thought of that poison, which is what I called it, entering his body had me feeling unsettled but I did not share how I was feeling about the chemo with him. I did not want to dissuade him from taking it because it was his body and his life, so I wanted him to do what he thought was best for him.

We had to go to Dr. Anderson to set up chemo and he wanted to approach the cancer aggressively, so he recommended that Vincent be admitted to the hospital to take three 36-hour treatments of chemo with each treatment taking place three weeks apart. The treatments were to start immediately. Vincent brought the video camera to the hospital and I do not know why he wanted to have this event on video, but I'm glad he did because it is the best footage we have of him. I was the one behind the camera and he was my subject. After Vincent was admitted to the hospital, he asked me to start recording him: "Good morning, everybody. Today is Monday, March the 4th. I'm just checking in and I'm 'bout to get a port today and tomorrow we'll start with chemo. We just gon document this process and see how it goes. Maybe nice some days and not so nice other days, but we'll get through it. God bless." Dr. Anderson had informed us of some side effects of chemo such as loss of appetite, mouth sores, hair loss and nausea. Vincent did not know how he would respond to it, but he knew that there was the possibility of some rough days ahead.

Vincent was admitted into the hospital on Monday, but the procedure for the port was not done until early Tuesday morning because he had to fast for 24 hours before the procedure. Therefore, the chemo did not begin until Wednesday. After the procedure, the attendant returned Vincent to the room. He was alert and ready to eat and I began recording. "Hello, everyone. You see that table over there? I'm 'bout to destroy that food." He had me turn the camera towards the food on the table. There were two hospital meals along with food I had prepared for him; and although he gave it a good try, he could not eat it all.

The following day the chemo began and for the first 24 hours, he was fine. Then I noticed him begin to slow down with his eating and he didn't have much of an appetite. "Eat, Papa, eat," I said as I pressed him to keep eating, but his appetite just wasn't there. In the recording he said, "Hello, everyone. Well, today is Friday, day five and I went smack dead into the wall. Don't feel like eating but I'm almost finished with the chemo. The last bag is up there and then they will put me on this other stuff to kind of help flush it out. But yeah, no appetite, hiccupping all day. Not feeling the best, but I'm doing alright."

Then he began to feel nauseous and the vomiting started. He was constantly up vomiting for most of the night. My husband had never been sick in the way of not feeling well throughout this whole cancer process until now. The chemo made him feel awful. He could barely lift his head up and there was nothing I could do to make him feel better except be there with him. Vincent and I finally left the hospital that Saturday morning. Dr. Anderson did not inform us about the possibility of hiccups but they started before we left the hospital, and they were relentless. The only time he would stop with the hiccups is if we were making love, which we did the first night home from the hospital. Vincent's sex drive never decreased and after we made love that first night, I said, "You didn't hiccup at all while we were making love."

"I know," he said. The hiccups lasted for about a week and then they were gone, thank God. I remember him whispering, "Lo, no hiccups." Putting my finger up to my mouth, I motioned for him to keep quiet as if the hiccups could hear us because I did not want them to start again. He slowly began to get his appetite back as it was nearing time for him to go for the second cycle.

Vincent checked into the hospital for the second cycle of chemo: "Good morning, everybody. Well, I am back again," he said as I began the recording. By this time, Vincent had started losing facial hair and the edges along his hair line. During the recording, I told him to turn to the sides so I could zoom in to get a good picture of his hair loss.

"The mustache is gone," I said.

And he asked, "Where is it? I don't know if that's the medicine or Loretta."

We both laughed as I said, "Loretta's been around forever and you ain't loss no hair."

"I'm trying to figure out which one is it," he said still laughing. The nurse prepared his port for the chemo drugs. As soon as the drugs were delivered to the room, the nurse came and started the IV drip and because of our experience with the first cycle, we knew what to expect this time. Like the first cycle, Vincent had a great appetite in the beginning; and he took daily walks this time, walking for about thirty minutes each day, sometimes twice a day. While pushing the IV pole, he walked about fifteen laps around the hospital floor. I walked with him for a couple of laps sometimes, and then I waited in the room for him to finish. Vincent walked at such a brisk pace that I could hear the rattling from the wheels of the IV pole before seeing him racing around the corner headed up the halls again for another lap.

On day three of the second chemo cycle, Vincent's appetite had waned and he began to feel nauseous. The hiccups started again but for the second cycle of chemo, Dr. Anderson had prescribed him medicine to help with the hiccups so they were not as relentless as the first time. He would hiccup for a while then stop and start up again later. Day four he began throwing up and said everything tasted and smelled like medicine. He took a shower to see if that would take the smell away and it helped a little because he felt somewhat better, but he still tasted and smelled the medicine in everything. After the second cycle of chemo was completed, the nurse started the IV flush. That night, he threw up what seemed like every hour and by the following morning, he was so weak; and just like in the first cycle, he could barely hold his head up. Head hung down, sitting on the edge of the bed, he said, "I'm ready to go home." We had to wait for the labs to come back to make sure his potassium level was where it should be; it was fine so we went home. The recovery process from the chemo drugs started again: hiccups, no appetite, and the new thing this time was the black spots on his tongue and in his mouth. He had to gargle with warm salt water and that helped with the discomfort.

Before starting the third cycle of chemo, Vincent called Dr. Shands to have an MRI done to see if the chemo was shrinking the tumor. "Lo, I'm not gonna keep taking that poison if it is not helping me," he said. In a way, I was glad that he did not want to take the chemo because it was difficult to see him feeling so awful after the chemo cycles and I never really wanted him to do chemo in the first place. However, the abysmal prognosis of the arm amputation did not set well with me either, so I did not know which was worse. Dr. Shands agreed to Vincent's request and ordered an MRI to see if the chemo was affecting the tumor in any way.

Vincent went in for the scheduled MRI and afterwards, he had an appointment to review the results. "The tumor is not shrinking; in fact, it has gotten larger," Dr. Shands said. He went on to say, "I can go back in and peel the layers off like I did before..."

But before he could complete what he was saying, Vincent abruptly interrupted him and said, "You can go ahead and amputate the arm."

Seeming to swallow the words he was planning to say, Dr. Shands said, "I have no problem amputating the arm if that's what you want me to do." I still see the look on the doctor's face. It was a look of not expecting Vincent to say what he said but pleased that Vincent chose that course of action without him having to explain or convince him that he believed that was the best course to take.

While they were talking, I was silently screaming, "No, wait a minute!" I wanted to tell Dr. Shands to go on with what he was saying about peeling the layers off but from the tone of Vincent's response, it was obvious he had given it much thought. It just all happened too fast for me. One second the doctor was talking about another surgery to remove the tumor and the next second, Vincent's saying go ahead and amputate the arm with no discussion or anything. I had no idea he would suggest amputation before the doctor did. We talked about it, but I didn't know he had come to that conclusion. "Amputate your arm, Vincent?" I asked after the doctor left the room.

"Yeah, Lo, I don't want the cancer to spread to my lungs because they say if it spreads to my lungs, there is nothing more that can be done," he answered. Obviously, he had kept the statement in mind that Dr. Shands had made about the spreading of the cancer to his lungs. I agreed with him because I did not want the cancer to spread to his lungs either, but I still wrestled with the thought of him only having one arm.

While waiting for the doctor to come back into the room, Vincent asked, "Lo, with only one arm, how will I tie my shoes?" Of all the situations he would have to adjust to by having one arm, he thought about how he was going to tie his shoes. Tying his shoes seemed trivial to me but it was obvious he had thought about it.

Without thinking about it, I jokingly said, "I guess you will have to get the shoes with velcro on them." We both laughed about it and the mood in the room was lightened because it was heavy for me. I was hoping he would not have to lose his arm. Dr. Shands wanted to do the surgery as soon as possible, which would have been the following Thursday. However, we let him know that Fantasy was graduating from college on that day and we did not want to miss her graduation, so he scheduled the surgery for the Thursday after that.

Fantasy graduated May 2, 2013, with her Bachelor of Arts in elementary education specializing in reading. My husband and I were so thankful for what she had accomplished. Fantasy was a diligent worker and always did well in school. She had a big setback with her health and a couple of other detours along the way, but she did not allow that to deter her from accomplishing her goal of graduating from college. We shared the news with our kids that their dad had decided to have his arm amputated, but we asked them not to tell anyone until after Fantasy's graduation. We decided that would be best because we did not want the news to put a damper on her celebration. Vincent did call Victor to inform him of the surgery and he also informed our pastor and that was it as far as family and friends were concerned until after Fantasy's graduation. To celebrate Fantasy's graduation, we invited friends and family to meet us later that evening at Red Lobster for dinner. There were about 20 of us gathered at the restaurant laughing, talking, eating, and then laughing and talking some more. No one else knew, not even his family, that he had decided to have his arm amputated. It was not until after Fantasy's graduation celebration that we began telling others about Vincent's decision.

Victor was planning to come to the states for his summer vacation but when Vincent told him he was having the surgery, he came a month early so he could be here with Vincent when he had the surgery. Victor was not here for Fantasy's graduation, so he must have arrived that weekend because we all went bowling the Sunday evening before the surgery. Bowling was a family event we often did together on Sunday evenings, and Vincent and our sons were good at it and very competitive. Vincent wanted to go bowling because he was not sure if he would be able to participate again in that activity he enjoyed doing with his family after the arm amputation, so we all met at the bowling alley. It was me, Vincent, Victor, Vincent Jr., Fantasy, Delrick, Tamika, and our granddaughters. The evening was like a party. We took pictures to have memories of what might have been the last time we would get to see Vincent's bowling swagger. Each time he went to roll the bowl, he did the same motions: picked up his ball, wiped it down with a towel, walked to a certain spot, hesitated with ball in position, and took the same number of steps, before confidently rolling the ball down the alley knowing he had either a strike or would have to clean up with a spare.

Getting ready for Fantasy's graduation helped to keep my mind occupied so I did not think much about Vincent's impending surgery. However, after Fantasy graduated, the surgery was all I thought about and I could not reconcile with it in my spirit. The inner turbulence I felt would not subside. I was not ready for the surgery, and I let God and my husband know that I was not ready. A few days before the surgery, I said, "Vincent, call Dr. Shands and ask can they take another MRI to see if the tumor is still there," because I was expecting God to do something miraculous. I thought the cancer thing was going a little too far and I was not comfortable with where it was going.

Vincent said, "Okay, I'll call," and he did. He spoke with Dr. Shands' nurse and said, "My wife asked me to call to see if you all could take another MRI to make sure the tumor is still there." Vincent said her response was, "Aww, tell her it's still there; it's not going anywhere." She also said she understood my concerns, but she was sure it was still there.

"How could she be so sure without taking another MRI?" I asked him. I understood from a medical position of her certainty, but I knew that God could eradicate the tumor if He willed to do so. I was expecting a 'late in the midnight hour' moment from God and perhaps that was the time for it, but I did not push the issue and her response did nothing to ease the turbulence I was feeling. Seeing an arm amputee was not a normal everyday occurrence for me and Vincent was the most active, competitive, athletic person I had ever known. When he played basketball with our sons and their friends, he ran circles around them. How was he going to adjust to having one arm? Or the bigger question was, how was I going to adjust to him having one arm? He seemed at peace with it. I was the one not willing to accept that he had to have his arm amputated. This was toiling in my spirit and it would not stop.

Two days before the surgery, I was at Sam's Club with our three granddaughters Lauryn, Morgan, and Aniston. As I was walking in the entrance to the store with the surgery on my mind, I was silently talking to God. "Lord, you've got to help me. I don't want to have to do this. What is it gonna look like? I don't see people with amputated arms; that's not normal," I said. As soon as I finished silently asking God for help, I looked and saw a man and woman walking who I assumed were husband and wife, and the man had one of his arms amputated. I cried out, "Thank you, Jesus! Thank you, Jesus!"

Our granddaughters asked, "Grandma what happened?" They didn't know I was silently having a conversation with God about their granddad's arm amputation. I showed them the man and the woman, and I told them what I had asked God.

"And then I saw that couple and the man has one of his arms amputated like granddad is going to have," I said. I was excitedly thankful, and I couldn't wait to tell my husband what happened. God allowing me to see that couple at that moment took away all the toil and turbulence in my spirit. I had a peace concerning the surgery that I didn't think I would ever have. When I saw my husband, I said, "I'm ready!" and I told him what happened at Sam's. He had the biggest grin on his face while I was talking to him. I believed that was a relief for him as well, because he knew I was not on board before. From that time until the amputation, I was ready with no hesitation.

The following day, which was Wednesday, my sister Gail called and said, "Lo, me and my girls put something together and we want to come by and honor that faith Vincent has. It's not much, just a little something we put together." Later that evening, Gail and her daughters came by the house and brought three heart-shaped pillows they had made in assorted sizes and colors. The smallest pillow was red, the next size was purple, and the largest pillow was gold. As they began to do their presentation, I saw the effort that they put into it, so I had them to wait while I grabbed the video camera. Vincent stood as Gail began to speak while her daughters Briana, China, and Curynn placed hearts around Vincent's neck in that order. "We did a red heart and it represents the love that we have for you; and we know the love that you have for God and the man of God that you are. Then we have the purple heart and that's just the courage and faith that we see, you just trusting God and believing God. Our hearts were broken and we didn't know what to say, but we knew that you trusted God and that's what kept us going. Even when I would call my sister or she would call me and I would say, 'Well, Lo, I know y'all got to be done felt the brunt of everything before you call us because how can you take all this?'

For courage and the faith, I thought about the purple heart because in the army that is how their courage is honored. And then the gold heart, it just represents the glory of God that we see on your life, how you can keep smiling and be so joyful. I don't know but I just thought about Jesus in the garden of Gethsemane, knowing that you're human and that you have feelings. And Jesus said, 'If it's possible, take this cup from me, Father; but nevertheless, not my will but thou will be done.' I know that's what you believe; I know that's what you say. So it helps us and it keeps us going and I just wanted to let you know that we are with you, we're praying for you, and we love you."

Vincent and Gail embraced each other, and he responded with, "I love all y'all. I want to say to my family, I love all y'all and I also believe that this is the will of God for my life; and I am willing to accept it and I am willing to trust God. I don't know what's happening at the end, but I know God has given me peace and assurance that He is in full control, and I am able to do that by the grace of God. So I trust God and believe Him. I am proud of all y'all and thank y'all; y'all mean a whole lot to me."

"And you mean a lot to us. We just wanted to honor you. That kind of faith and courage needed to be honored some kind of way, so we went elementary style," Gail said as she touched the pillows and we all laughed. She may have thought that was elementary style but for us, it was grand and we knew that the glory was God's and belonged to Him. Not only did she come to honor the faith and courage she saw in Vincent but she got her daughters involved as well, which says a lot because her girls were grown women at the time and they agreed to take some time and come with their mom to honor their uncle Vincent in that way. Later that evening, Vincent's mom and siblings came to the house. We talked, laughed, and took pictures because Vincent wanted to have pictures of him and his family on the final evening that he still had both arms. It was the atmosphere of a celebration, knowing that through all of this, we were trusting God. The evening was great preparation for the impending events of the next day.

Chapter 14

We Ready!

Vincent had to be at the hospital at 6:45am, so we had to leave our house by 4:00am to arrive at the hospital in Gainesville on time. Vincent, me, Delrick, Fantasy, Vincent Jr., Victor and our nephew Markitis, loaded two vehicles and headed to Shands Hospital to be there for Vincent's surgery. Before we left the house for Gainesville, I began to record Vincent saying, "Well, today is May 9th, 2013. Gotta head to Gainesville for my surgery. This is the last couple of hours that I'll have my left shoulder. So thank you, Jesus, and I pray that everything go alright and I will be back home soon and we'll have the end of this cancer thing. God bless you."

"Alright, anybody else wanna say something?" I asked.

"No, I'm too emotional," Victor said as he just waved to the camera. Before leaving, we all gathered in a circle, held hands, and prayed. Then we did fist bumps while asking each other, "You ready?" with everyone responding, "Yeah."

"Okay, let's do this," I said as we headed out the door. I felt as if we were going up against an opponent and whatever the outcome was, we win with God. Victor was emotional and I understood that because if I had not received what I believed to be an "It's okay" moment from God, I know I would have been an emotional wreck. But God had given me peace and strength that even bewildered me. There was no hesitation anywhere in me, only the desire for Vincent to have the surgery because I believed God had confirmed to me that it was all right.

When we arrived at the hospital, Vincent had to prepare to have a nerve block put in and the doctor had to make sure the nerve block was working before the surgery. They took us to a room where he had to undress and put on a hospital gown and hair net. I started recording and he said, "Oops, don't show my butt," as he grabbed the back of the gown to make sure it was closed, and we both started laughing. Thankfully, the mood was not gloomy at all. The nerve block was successful and they prepared to take Vincent back to surgery. We all told him we love him and we'll see him after the surgery. After we gave kisses and fist bumps, we went to the surgery waiting area. The kids brought a deck of cards with them, and they played cards to pass the time while Vincent was in surgery.

The surgery lasted about four hours and afterwards, Dr. Shands came out and told us the surgery was over and we could see Vincent shortly. "And the tumor was still there," he said because his nurse told him about Vincent's phone call regarding my request of taking another MRI to confirm that the tumor was still there.

"Oh, I am fine now," I said, and I excitedly told him of the incident that happened when I was in Sam's Club and how I was talking to God just before I saw the man with the amputated arm.

"Wow, that's great!" he said. He also said, "You all be ready when he gets home. I have never had a patient who didn't hit a wall after that type of surgery."

We looked at him with some concern and said, "Okay," because I could see the possibility of that happening after a life-changing surgery of a limb amputation.

"Can I see the arm?" Victor asked.

"No," the doctor responded and he explained why Victor couldn't see the arm. I thought it was a rather odd request because seeing Vincent's arm after the amputation seemed a bit gruesome to me.

I in no way wanted to see his arm not attached to his body, but I'm sure Victor had his reason for wanting to see it.

After waiting a little while, we were finally allowed to go back and see Vincent. He was still in recovery, and I did not know how I would react or how he would react. I did not have concern, but I did not know what to expect when I got a chance to see him after the surgery. Also, I didn't want to give a reaction to upset him. Feeling a little anxious, I went in to see him; and when I did, the strength and peace God had given me was still there. "Hey, bae," I said as I walked into his recovery room. He was still heavily under the influence of anesthesia. The amputation site was tightly wrapped with an ace bandage.

He opened his eyes and groggily said, "Hey."

"Hey, bae, I love you," I said as I leaned forward and kissed him. "How ya feeling?" I asked.

"I'm okay," he responded. Because he was still under the influence of the anesthesia, I did not say much. I told him I was going to let the others come see him, because everyone except Victor and I were driving back to Sanford that evening. Victor was staying at a hotel in Gainesville and I was staying with Vincent at the hospital. They each went in one at a time to see Vincent and then they left. The kids headed home and Victor went to his hotel room. The nurses told me that Vincent's room was ready and if I wanted to, I could wait in his room and they would be bringing him in shortly. The attendant brought Vincent to the room and made sure he had him hooked up to the IV meds he needed before he left.

"You want me to record you, bae?" I asked.

"Yeah," he said. As he lay comfortably in the bed still a little groggy, he began to say, "Hello, everybody, I've had the surgery and I give God all the praise because He has given me strength, He has given me peace, and He gave me a beautiful wife. I want to say thank you,

Lo, for being there for me, standing with me, and just giving me strength also so I can go through this. I thank all my family, the Paiges' and the Gilchrists'. And I'm kind of tired right now because the medicine is still working on me, but I have enough sense to give God all the praise." For about two minutes, we both began to worship and praise God because we knew that it was only by His grace that we were able to endure. After that, Vincent was tired so he went to sleep. I prepared the pullout bed for me to lay down, and I dozed off to sleep too because it had been a long day.

The following morning, Vincent walked to the bathroom with the nurse at his side for added stability after the surgery. He walked with no problem and afterwards, he sat in the chair to eat breakfast. As he sat in the chair eating breakfast, I began recording him: "Hello, it's Friday morning, the day after surgery. I'm doing alright, trying to get something to eat to make my stomach feel better. Other than that, I got up and walked today, so praise God."

By that time, Victor had arrived at the hospital and he interjected, "He's doing good though. I saw his backside there and he needs a little lotion, but he's doing good though."

With the three heart shaped pillows that Gail and her daughters presented to him hanging on his IV pole, Vincent and Victor went for a walk later that afternoon. Vincent was still feeling the effects of the medicine and he hoped the walk would aid in working the medicine out of his system. As I think about how I felt after the surgery, Vincent not having his left arm anymore was not an issue for me. I don't remember giving it much thought. Vincent was always so strong and he quickly bounced back from the surgery. I am so thankful Victor came a month earlier than usual for the summer so he could be there for the surgery as well. Vincent had a great relationship with his other siblings, but there was something special about the 'twins' relationship. Although Victor lived in another country, Vincent communicated with him more than he did with his siblings who lived in the same city. There was mutual respect and understanding between Vincent and Victor. They disagreed, debated with each other, sometimes agreeing to disagree, but never held grudges. It was a loving, healthy sibling relationship and throughout the process, Victor was there.

Vincent was released from the hospital the Monday after his surgery. Before his release, the nurse came in and removed the bandages so she could remove the drain tube. "Take a deep breath," the nurse said as she removed the tube. Vincent grimaced in pain as the tube came out saying, "Ayyyyy." After the nurse finished, Vincent said, "That hurt, I wasn't expecting that." Dr. Shands came in later and looked over the surgery area; he was pleased with what he saw. He closed the incision with surgery glue, and he said the glue would dissipate eventually. The surgery area looked good, but I didn't expect most of his shoulder to be gone. I thought it was an 'arm' amputation, but half his shoulder was gone on that left side. We left the hospital and during the ride home, I told Vincent what the doctor said about him hitting a wall. "I am not hitting a wall. Why would I hit a wall?" he said.

"Dr. Shands said he has never had a patient with the type of surgery you had who has not hit a wall and that we should be ready," I told him.

"Well, I'm gonna be the first to not hit a wall," Vincent said.

After we arrived home, Vincent took off all the bandages as he prepared to take a shower. Victor was not in the room with us when the nurse removed the bandages or when the doctor came in to see the surgery area so when we arrived home, that was the first time he saw Vincent without the bandages on. While I recorded, Vincent began to say: "Okay, we're home and as you can see this is my first time actually seeing what was done." He turned from one side to the other, so the viewers would be able to see the entire surgery area. "That was a major surgery, but I'm doing good a couple of days afterwards. God is good, so we just bless Him and thank Him for bringing me through," he said while flexing his right arm. "Alright, time to wash," Vincent went on to say and moving his right hand as if he was bathing he went on to say, "Got to get all this iodine, betadine, and all this other stuff off me." Then he turned to Victor, gave him a fist bump and asked, "We okay? You good?"

Then Victor turned toward the camera and said, "Whoa," with an astonished look on his face. "This is my first time seeing it too and he's doing great though; but looks like they cut him in half, but he'll get back. This is a strong man right here; a strong man and I love him to death."

While giving another fist bump Vincent said, "I love you too man." He went on to say, "Alright, Dr. Paige, we'll get back in the gym and start working out."

Vincent knew that seeing the amputation site was shocking for Victor because he himself said, "That's something to see." I am convinced that the reason Vincent said he and Victor would get back in the gym soon was to encourage Victor because he did not want him to worry about him, and that is exactly what they did. When we went to the follow-up appointment after the surgery, Vincent asked Dr. Shands about the amputation because we did not know he was cutting as much off his shoulder as he did. He told us it was a forequarter shoulder amputation. I am sure he told us that before the surgery but for some reason, I had an arm amputation in my mind and never questioned what a forequarter shoulder amputation was. Vincent requested copies of all his medical records and scans. He was studious about looking up information on the Internet about the different procedures he had to endure. I was surprised he did not research a forequarter shoulder amputation so that we would have some idea of what it would look like.

A week into Vincent's recovery, our son Delrick and his family came over for a visit and our grandkids and I went to the tennis courts which was just steps away from our apartment. Vincent came outside with us and I began to feed the two oldest girls the tennis ball as they took turns hitting it across the net. At that time, they were only eight, six, and five years of age. Delrick came outside with the video camera and recorded us as Vincent and I often did when we had our grandkids. With his cane for extra support, Vincent kicked the ball if they missed it while he was playing with the youngest grand who was playing with a basketball on the court at the same time. As she was dribbling the ball, he was sticking his foot out to kick at it. I was paying close attention to him because I did not want him to stumble and fall. At first, I was a little nervous but once I saw that he kept his balance and he had his strength, the nervousness subsided. That was the first time since the surgery that he was involved in any kind of outdoor physical activity, and he enjoyed it.

About two weeks after the surgery, Vincent started walking around our apartment complex. Victor and I would not let him walk alone so if I did not walk with him, Victor did. The first time he set out to go walking after the surgery, he did not say anything. I just happened to see him putting on his sneakers so I asked, "Where you going?"

"I'm 'bout to go walking," he answered.

"Not by yourself," I responded as I hurried to put on walking clothes and my sneakers to go with him. I was not worried about him not being able to walk, I was worried about him overdoing it because I knew he wanted to get back to his old self as soon as he could. He wanted to get back to doing activities he enjoyed.

Vincent began by walking around the complex four times. Then he built up to six times, which was about three miles. Victor and I hung in there with him for about two weeks but after we saw that his walks went well and he did not have any problems, we let him go solo (but we still checked on him). Victor and I waited a couple of minutes and then one of us went to the porch to wait for him to pass by. "How many is that?" I asked Vincent.

"Four; two more to go," Vincent responded as he continued walking without breaking stride. Vincent was not much of a walker; he was more of a runner. His normal workout was a two-mile run and twenty to thirty minutes of lifting weights, which he did about four times a week. After his six-week checkup, he and Victor got back to the gym as he said and he also started playing tennis again.

Vincent and Victor were outside playing tennis one day and I heard Vincent yell, "Gotcha! Don't play with me. Woohoo!" as he pumped his tennis racquet up and down in his arm signaling that he had scored.

"Your advantage," Victor said calling out the score.

Victor served and Vincent won the next point. "Woohoo, 6-3!" Vincent yelled again. "Poogy, you wanna play your uncle? I done beat him and now you can beat him," he said boastfully. "I don't want to hear no excuse," Vincent said rubbing it in to Victor that he beat him. He and Victor were very competitive, and they both wanted to win. Victor never won a set playing tennis against Vincent but since Vincent had only one arm, I think Victor thought that was his chance.

"Naw, man I'm warmed up now," Victor said.

"Oh, you wanna play again? Come on, let's play again. He cannot beat me!" Vincent said emphatically. After taking a few minutes to rest, drink some Gatorade, and argue about how the first set was scored, they played again.

"Even before he lost his arm, he used to beat up on me so that's nothing new. He didn't lose both his arms," Victor said.

"Hey, Poogy, I need a witness. What did he say? He said he's gon kick my butt?" Vincent asked.

"I'll say it again: I'm gon kick your ah, ah," Victor said and they headed to the court.

To serve the ball, Vincent put the ball on his tennis racquet, tossed it up off his racquet and then hit the ball as it came down. Vincent won that set 6-0. Afterwards, they had post-set comments for the camera: "I just want to thank the fans for being behind me and the support I get from my wife. It was a hard-fought match but as I predicted, I prevailed and beat him six, zip," Vincent said.

Victor replied, "Well the thing is that he's my brother and I'm trying to get him back into shape, so this was a moral victory for him. I let him get out there and do some things that I shouldn't have let him do. I take this defeat in grace. He beat me six, zip and um, I'm smoking a cigarette," while taking a pull from his cigarette.

"I just would like to say once again..." Vincent started.

Then Victor interrupted, "Naw, you said what you said; you don't talk no more. It went to you and then it went to me; that's it."

"The champ got to have the last word," Vincent said.

"And the first word and in between word," Victor commented.

"Exactly," Vincent responded. "I am still the heavy weight reigning champion of the tennis court. Thank you very much," Vincent said.

"And I'm gon leave it at that. Peace," Victor said while making the peace sign as they both laughed.

After six weeks of recovery from the arm amputation surgery, Vincent returned to work despite some suggesting that he apply for disability. The only concern Vincent had about going back to work was whether or not he could return to his old position of the lead in shipping and receiving because it involved driving a fork lift which was steered with the left hand. Vincent had worked at his place of employment for almost 20 years and he and his coworkers had mutual respect and appreciation for each other. Vincent called those he worked with his Invacare family because he said, "I am with them eight, sometimes ten hours a day and it's like we are family." Invacare was so supportive of him throughout the entire ordeal. When he had to take leave from work for chemo treatments or surgeries, there was never an issue and he was always welcomed back. When he returned to work after the surgery, the concern about the forklift was eradicated because Invacare had a forklift that he was able to steer with his right hand. His excitement about the right-handed forklift was on display as he said, "God had them to have that forklift there just for me!"

Vincent had been back to work for a few weeks when he started complaining about pain in his left arm which bewildered me because how could he have pain in his left arm if his left arm was not there. I could not understand that, but he insisted that there was definitely pain in his left arm. "It's not painful all the time but every now and then, I feel it," he said.

After describing the pain to the doctor, his response was, "It's called phantom pain, and it is real." He went on to prescribe Vincent medication that he said should help with the pain. Vincent took the medication as prescribed and it stopped the pain. Each morning, he made sure he took his medication with him when he went to work. I was not used to getting up at 5:30am but after Vincent's arm amputation, I had to get up with him as he prepared for work. I helped him with tying his shoes, making sure he had his medication for the phantom pain and with packing lunch if he decided to take leftovers from the previous night. Before his arm amputation, he took great care not to disturb my sleep as he prepared for work such as closing the bathroom door so the light would not shine in the bedroom, and he prepared his attire for work the night before. However, after the arm amputation, he left the bathroom door open and shined the light in the bedroom because he wanted to wake me. With my eyes adjusting to the light, I would look up and see him beckoning me with his hand to get up. It was never easy for me to get up that early, but I knew he needed my assistance.

With my birthday approaching in June, I told Vincent I wanted to go dancing. We had not been dancing in a while, so I let him know that was my desire and he agreed. By this time, Victor's daughter Sibel was also here from Turkey for the summer. While Victor had been here for almost two months already, Sibel had to wait for the school year to end before she came to the states. I told our children our plans for my birthday, and they thought it was a good idea. I also invited my sisters and his sisters to join us as well. It was like a celebration for us that we needed after the last eighteen months. We decided to go to BB King's for dinner and dancing. Our party included Vincent, me, Delrick and Tamika, Fantasy, Vincent Jr., Victor, Sibel, my sisters Jonita and Gail, and Vincent's sisters Lisa, and Stacy. I was so thankful that our family members came with us to celebrate not only my birthday, but also to celebrate Vincent and what he endured.

When we arrived at BB King's, we were seated on the upper level overlooking the dance floor. After ordering and eating our dinner over conversation and laughter, Vincent and I headed for the dance floor to dance the night away. The dance floor was crowded at times and at other times, it was just me and him. His arm amputation did not hinder his dance moves either, only he had to hold me with one arm now instead of two. Whether with one arm or with both arms, dancing with him was spirited bliss because he was my audience, and I was his.

Chapter 15

The Paige Family Reunion

The Thursday following my birthday was the 4th of July and for that weekend, Vincent's family planned a much-needed family reunion beginning on that Thursday and ending on Saturday. It had been over 39 years since he and his siblings had been altogether in one place at the same time. Vincent was one of fifteen children between his mother and his father. His mother had two daughters, Vernisa and Denise, before her and his father met; and his father also had two other children, Willie and Karen. Vernisa, Denise, Willie, and Karen were not raised in the same household as Vincent and the other kids. The ones raised by their mother and father included six boys, Tony, Eric, Dale, Vincent, Victor, Stanley, and three girls, Inez, Lisa, and Stacy. Vincent's parents also had another set of twins who passed away shortly after birth. Vernisa was raised by his mother's aunt and Denise was raised by his mother's mom. Vincent did not meet Willie until he came to live in Florida as an adult and he knew of Karen, but he did not meet her until he went to his father's funeral. Karen came to town for the reunion as well but unfortunately, his stepbrother Willie had passed away a few years earlier after an illness.

I could not clearly recall the details Vincent shared with me as to why it took 39 years for his mom and siblings to get together, so I asked Victor, and this is what he penned for me:

In 1974, Vince and I were nine years old. Mom left Pop with the help of Jimmie Lee, Pop's brother. He drove us to the bus station, and we were off to Sanford, Florida. When we arrived, we stayed with Uncle

James, Mom's brother, and we hated it because to us, Uncle James was mean, and he looked scary too. He had an old lady staying with him who we thought was an old witch. Anyway, all of us staying with Uncle James was not working out. It was too crowded, and he did not want us there either. Denise was also staying there with us.

Fast forward, Mom got a house for us, and Grandma stayed with us, but Denise did not. Vernisa came to America because she had been in Germany with her husband Wyzee, who was in the military. That was the first time that we met her. Funny because I can remember a popular song that was out during that time, "I Believe in Miracles, You Sexy Thing." She stayed in Sanford for a couple of days, but I only remember her coming over to the house that one time and then again right before she left. Everything was going fine for about eight months or longer. We were in school, Mom was working, and it seemed like we had finally escaped Pop's torture for good. But what we did not know was that Pop had found a way to contact Mom and Mom told no one. Pop had started writing letters to Mom trying to convince her that he had changed. Well, that sh*t worked and finally Mom told us that we were going back. Everyone was furious and no one wanted to go back. Pop sent Mom bus fare for her to bring us back, but not all of us. He specifically wanted the little ones and Tony to come back. The little ones were from Inez down to Stanley, so Eric and Dale stayed in Sanford.

When we came back home with Pops, we lived above a pool hall and there was not enough space there for seven kids, so Vince and I had to live with Uncle Jimmie Lee. Pop never knew that his brother helped us leave and I hate to think what would have happened if he had found out. One of them would probably have died and that's real. We stayed there for a while until Pop got mad at Uncle Jimmie Lee and made us go stay with his girlfriend, Pat. Pat was a nice lady too and she stayed close to the hospital where Pop worked. We could see the hospital from her front window. Vince and I went to a school not too far from Pat's house and after school, we had to come straight back to Pat's house. But we would walk to the pool hall to see Mom and everyone, then walk thirty minutes back to Pat's house. Pop never got angry about that, so we did it quite often.

By 1976, we were all back at the pool hall and Eric and Dale had come back too. Pop bought a house in 1977, because he had an accident at the hospital where he worked, and he took a settlement. Eric saved his money from summer jobs and moved back to Florida. Later, Tony joined the Army. One summer, Inez had a fight with Mom and pulled a knife on her. She thought she could take Mom and she thought wrong. Mom was whipping her a** in fighting, so she grabbed a knife. Mom called Pop and Pop came looking for her. If Pop had found her, he would have beaten her so badly that I'm sure she would have had to go the hospital and stay for a couple of days. Also, when we found out, we were looking for her to beat her a** too. So, Inez could not stay at the house anymore. Grandma sent for Inez to come to Sanford and stay with her. Then, there was only Dale, Vince and me at the house.

When Lisa, Stacey, and Stanley got sent away, it changed Pop. He stopped beating us. Dale was getting bigger, and Vince and I were around twelve and I can't remember getting a beating from Pop again. He would still beat Mom sometimes, but not as much as he did in the past. He threatened to beat us when he thought we got out of line, but he wouldn't beat us anymore. During all that time, Vernisa wrote letters to Mom occasionally, maybe once or twice a year, but she or Denise never really stayed in contact with any of us. Dale graduated from high school and got tired of going to the pool hall every day after work and on the weekends, so he found himself a job and moved out. Then it was only Vince and me at the house. Mom had a job at the Holiday Inn, and she would give Vince and I an allowance before Pop came and took her money.

About a month before Vince and I were leaving to go to college, Child Services gave Lisa, Stacey, and Stanley back to Mom. Inez *came to visit with her first-born son and Pop liked him so much. He was also Pop's first grandson. Pop tried to get Inez to leave him in Rochester with him and Mom, but of course, Inez would not. Also, during that time, Tony got out of the army, but he started getting in trouble and he went to prison. Vincent and I left in August of 1983 for Daytona Beach, Florida. Since everyone was trying to make it on their own, coming together was never talked about. Even Vince and I never talked about all of us getting together, but I think it really became a thing once Vince was diagnosed with cancer. It seemed like the perfect time for all of us to get together since Tony was finally out of prison. I can still hear Vince saying, "39 years and finally all of Mom's children are together; never know if this will ever happen again." Well, he was right about that.*

After 39 years, the family reunion was long overdue. The event planned for Thursday was hosted by Vincent's sister Denise at her home with the siblings and their children. Vincent's mother had no idea that all of her eleven children were going to be there. She thought everyone was coming except her oldest daughter Vernisa. Everyone else knew Vernisa was coming and they wanted their mom to be surprised, so no one told her. While my mother-in-law was enjoying her other children and their families, Vernisa arrived from Alabama. Out of my mother-in-law's view, she exited her car and quietly tipped up behind my mother-in-law and tapped her on the shoulder. My mother-in-law turned around and when she saw Vernisa, she screamed and tightly embraced her for about ten seconds. She finally let go and waved her hands in the air in delight. Then she screamed and embraced her again as the other children looked on with big smiles knowing that their mom was elated to have all her children together in one place. My mother-in-law was happy to see Karen as well because she said she remembered keeping her when she was younger.

I so enjoyed seeing my husband around his family because I know how much he loved them and how important they were to him.

Vincent and Victor initiated the idea of a family reunion; the other ones thought it was a great idea and they were quickly on board. Vincent walked around with his video camera recording the various aspects of that day from the siblings playing cards and talking smack to each other to everyone enjoying the delicious food that was prepared for the day. The evening culminated with us all gathering at Stanley's house for the lighting of the fireworks.

The next two days, which were Friday and Saturday, the reunion plans involved more relatives from his father's side of the family. Cousin Ronnie, who is his aunt Alean's son, cousin Juanita, who is his uncle Joe's daughter, and Woody, who I'm still not sure how he was related, all traveled from Miami to Sanford for the family reunion. Vincent felt like his other relatives probably thought that this reunion was not going to happen because there were underlying thoughts and comments regarding Buddy Boy's children because he did not have close relationships with his own siblings. Vincent said his behavior and actions may have been attributed to him having PTSD from the time he was in the military. Although he was never officially diagnosed with it, it seemed like the obvious reason to Vincent for his father to behave the way he did.

Vincent told me that while growing up in Rochester, his dad did not allow their relatives to come to their home and they could not visit the homes of their relatives. Buddy Boy was often confrontational with his own siblings and did not want them at his home. Vincent also told me that when his father's mother died, his father made it mandatory for him and his siblings to attend the funeral but they could not ride with him or any other family member so they had to walk to the funeral and walk back home. Buddy Boy's children were kind of kept away from the rest of the family and he and Victor believe that is the reason they did not receive the support when they went off to college from their aunts and uncles in the same way that the other nephews and nieces received support. Because of this, Vincent was under the impression that there was not much regard for him and his siblings from his paternal relatives, and he said they probably thought none of them would ever amount to anything.

Vincent, Victor, Ronnie, and Juanita put in the work to make the family reunion happen the final two days. Vincent's cousin David and his wife lived in Altamonte Springs, Florida, in a home with a covered patio and pool, so they agreed to have the Friday evening festivities at his house. It was questioned by some of Vincent's paternal relatives as to whether certain ones of Buddy Boys sons would attend the reunion because of some inconsistencies in behavior. Proudly, I watched as all of Buddy Boy's children and their families, especially the boys, show up and make it a successful family reunion. They accounted for over 75% of the family that came.

Tony, who is the oldest, came walking up with his shades on and he was all business ready to make it happen. Then there's Eric, who came up talking loudly, like he usually does, ready to have a good time. Dale, following Eric, came in speaking to those he saw and seeing if there was something he could do to help those who were preparing for the evening. Vincent walked in behind Dale with the biggest smile on his face and with his video camera ready to get footage as he greeted those he saw with a hug. Victor walked in next, also smiling and greeting everyone. Then Stanley walked in smiling and speaking to those who were there. Stanley did not say much, but he was ready to go with the flow. Ronnie also had his camera taking pictures as we sat around the pool and ate fried fish, French fries, and salad that was prepared by Juanita. David and his wife came home from work to a full house and they both were still great hosts. They joined the other family members as if they had been there the entire time.

Vernisa and Denise did not come to the festivities on Friday evening, but Inez, Lisa, Stacy and Karen were there. I met one of Vincent's relatives and her fiancé from one of the Carolinas who was recovering from a car accident, and she had to have assistance with walking. Vincent and I had a pleasant conversation with them because we enjoyed talking about marriage to other married couples or those who were planning to marry. We knew that because of what God had given us in our marriage, it was not ours to keep to ourselves. We knew we had to share it with others and that is what we did whenever we had the chance to do it. Jynetra, the daughter of Vincent's cousin Jody was also at the reunion. Some of them had a spades card game going on while most of the kids were watching a show on the television. My mother-in-law was not saying much, but the smile she had on her face said it all.

Saturday was officially the last day of the Paige Family reunion and an afternoon cookout at the park was the planned event. Everyone attended this cookout, including Vernisa and Denise. Juanita prepared most of the sides while Ronnie brought most of the meat. There was plenty of food to eat and plenty of good times to have. Some of the guys played croquet with Vincent and he was so far ahead of them in the game that it afforded him to start clowning. With the mallet in his hand, he looked up to the sky and closed his eyes before hitting the ball through the hoop. Then he looked at the other players and laughed. Another time he even turned his back on the hoop and hit the ball between his legs with the mallet, and it went through the hoop. When he hit the ball through the last hoop, he jumped up and kicked his heels together in jubilation. It didn't matter if the activity was croquet or basketball, Vincent had fun but you had better believe he was in it to win it.

The kids had hula hoops which of course, some of the adults had to try too. Mico, Stanley's long-time girlfriend, showed off her young-girl moves as she kept the hula hoop circling her waist with what seemed like little effort at all. When some of the other adults tried it, they forgot to move their hips, and the hula hoop fell to the ground. While the kids continued to run around and play, the men sat around and laughed as they talked about old times, and the women began to put away the leftover food and clean the area under the gazebo. Sunday morning, Vincent and I went to Stanley's house after church to see Tony and Dale because they were leaving to go back to their homes. All the brothers were there, and they talked and reminisced about the fantastic time they had that weekend.

Chapter 16

Adjusting to Change

In a conversation after Vincent's amputation, Dr. Shands said, "In three months, we will scan; if there is no sign of the cancer, we will remove the port. I perceived that to mean he believed that if the scan was clear, then the cancer would not return. After three months, the scan showed no sign of cancer and the chemo port was removed. I thought surely we were done with the cancer. God clearly showed me that He was with us when He removed the inner turbulence I had with Vincent's impending amputation and gave me a peace about it that I did not think was possible. He had revealed to us that He was more than enough again just as He did with Fantasy's ordeal and I was hoping that was the end of the cancer.

Vincent did not slow down after his surgery. He thrived at his place of employment and in everyday life. He even went to the basketball court sometimes to play the sport he thoroughly enjoyed playing. He also began to gain a little weight, which I did not mind as long as he did not allow his weight to get out of hand. He was the heaviest I had ever seen him, which really was not heavy at all but I took notice of the weight gain. "Alright, you better not get fat on me. I don't want a one-arm fat man," I said jokingly and we both laughed.

Vacations had been few and far between after the cancer diagnosis, so we planned a weekend getaway in Clearwater. Fantasy got her first teaching assignment at a school about a thirty-minute drive from our home and since the school was on the way, we stopped in for a few minutes to see her before heading to Clearwater. School had not started yet, but Fantasy was in the process of setting up her classroom to prepare for the arrival of the students. We knew she was nervous and unsure about what she needed to do. With a look of uncertainty, she showed us her classroom and told us what her goal was and the reason behind the way she was arranging it. Also, she introduced us to the principal of the school and some of her colleagues. We encouraged her and assured her that we knew she was going to be a great teacher. After hugs and kisses, we continued traveling to Clearwater.

The hotel we stayed at in Clearwater was right on the beach. Once we stepped outside of the lobby, we stepped into the sand on the beach; it was beautiful as white lounge chairs adorned the blue water's edge. The sun shone brightly in the sky and its reflection on the water was like sparkling crystal. Also, the hotel's pool area was outside of the lobby as well. Neither of us were beach or sun people, but we put on our swim attire, found a couple of lounge chairs under a tree for shade, and relaxed for a while. With eyes closed, I lay in the lounge chair breathing in the tranquil atmosphere. I am sure Vincent did not close his eyes, because he was always watchful and aware of his surroundings; for that reason, I knew I could relax and close mine.

He often told me and the kids, "Always be aware of your surroundings and pay attention to what's going on around you." Vincent talked about how he used to stop to get coffee each morning at a convenience store near his job before going to work. "Lo, I'll be fixing my coffee but every time I hear the door chime, I look up to see who's coming in and where they're going while I continue to fix my coffee," he said while acting out what he does when holding the cup on the counter with one hand, stirring it with the other hand and lifting his head up to see who's coming in the door. To me it was hilarious, but he was serious about watching his surroundings.

I could hear kids playing and the noise of people laughing and talking, but it did not take away from the tranquility I felt. We laid out for about two hours and after going in and taking a shower, we had dinner. By this time, it was dark out and I wanted to do a little walking outside near the hotel. Vincent did not want to go walking which was surprising to me because when we went to Miami Beach, we often walked on Ocean Drive and the surrounding area after dinner. Since Clearwater Beach was similar, I asked him why he didn't want to go walking. "Lo, I can't protect you like I used to," he said.

"What do you mean, protect me?" I asked.

"Since I only have one arm now, I'm not able to do some things I could've done before," he said. Obviously, our thinking was not the same because I was only thinking about having a good time and doing activities we normally do, but Vincent was always thinking ahead; and with the changes he had in his body, he realized that he now had limitations, which meant changes in our activities. I knew he was my protector, but the thought of him not being able to protect me never crossed my mind. I did not know he was thinking about having to protect me, but he was. I was a little disappointed about not going for a walk, but I understood his concerns. We returned to our hotel room and enjoyed the rest of the evening. It was that night that I realized my husband's arm amputation was not just a physical change, but there were psychological changes as well, which was to be expected, but that was the first manifestation of it.

The following morning, we found a nice little breakfast spot that seemed popular because it was crowded; so much so that we had to wait for a table. The restaurant was not big or extravagant, but it was just a small little joint near the beach and the food was delicious. After breakfast, we took a relaxing walk on the beach, taking in the sun and the sounds of the ocean and stopping to take a few pictures as we were enjoying our time together. Later that evening, we drove south into Clearwater and discovered a seafood restaurant near the water.

Our table was next to a window that looked out on the ocean. I do not remember what Vincent had to eat, but I had a scallop salad and it came in a huge martini glass. The waiter brought the filled glass to our table, and he turned the glass upside down onto my plate. I could see that there was plenty of scallop salad in the glass; but when I lifted the martini glass off my plate, to my surprise, the salad was enormous and covered the entire plate. The salad was mounded up on my plate so high that it spilled over the side of the dish. The freshness of the scallops, the sweetness from the cubed mango, and the sharpness of the chopped red onions along with the greens in the salad made my taste buds dance. I wanted to eat all of it because it was too good not to, and salads do not make good leftovers. We sat and talked as we ate and enjoyed our dinner, and before I knew it, I had eaten all the salad; but I must say that I paid for it afterwards.

I remember doing that once before when we went to a Bubba Gump restaurant in Miami and I had the bucket of shrimp, of which I consumed all of them and my stomach was in turmoil. Well, here it happened again; but afterwards, we went to a couple of stores before going back to the hotel and walking helped to ease the discomfort. It seemed like that much needed weekend getaway went by so fast but we enjoyed it to the fullest and the following morning, we returned home.

The church that we attended was having a Labor Day picnic and they asked me to make a homemade frozen dessert that, because of a lack of a better word, I call sherbet. Also, my family reunion is usually the weekend before Labor Day, commencing on Friday and ending on Sunday. But that year, it was just one day (Saturday), which worked out great for us because a lot of work goes into preparing for our three-day family reunion. There were times that if the church had a Labor Day picnic after our family reunion, I would not attend because of exhaustion; but Vincent never missed the church picnics. He always enjoyed being around the church members, talking, laughing, eating, and getting others involved in the games. He had more energy than the teenagers did. Whether he was hula hooping with the kids or playing volleyball with the adults, he just kept going. "You wanna play volleyball?" he asked different ones as he was getting his team together at the Labor Day picnic. "Can you play? Because if you can't play, you can't be on my team," he said and he meant it.

I had not seen him play volleyball since the surgery, so I was thinking, "Now here he is with one arm and he's asking others can they play? Can he play?" was my question. Well, I got my answer to that question because he went out there and played better than those who had two arms. He was out there running around setting up balls if he had to or hitting the balls over the net that someone set up for him. And of course, his team won.

Dr. Shands also recommended that Vincent get fitted for a prosthetic shoulder so that his shirts and suits would fit him better. Because most of his left shoulder was gone, when he put his shirts or his suit jackets on, I turned the sleeves inside and pinned them up from the inside so the sleeves did not hang off his shoulder. Pinning the shirt sort of simulated a shoulder. Vincent agreed to the prosthetic because he liked to dress and he wanted to look well put together. In fact, he ironed everything, even his handkerchiefs. Before going to bed each night of the work week, Vincent ironed his work shirts and his pants, which was habit for him. I would often grab a shirt and put it on without ironing it, and he would say, "Lo, take that shirt off and give it to me so I can iron it." To me, the shirt would be fine; but it wasn't good enough for him, so I'd take it off and let him iron it.

Finding out that they made prosthetics for the shoulder was surprising because I always thought of prosthetics for legs and arms; I had never met anyone with a forequarter shoulder amputation either. Even the man we saw in Sam's had an arm amputation but he still had his shoulder. It never crossed my mind that Vincent needed a prosthetic shoulder. In my mind, I pictured the arm and leg prosthetics with steel rods for the limbs, so I had no idea what a prosthetic shoulder was or what it looked like. There was not a prosthetic technician in Sanford, but one came from out of town to fit Vincent for the prosthetic shoulder. Dr. Shands contacted the prosthetic technician and he agreed to come to a medical supply office in Sanford. He sculpted a shoulder onto Vincent's left side with some type of material that hardened as it dried, like a cast. Vincent stood as the technician layered the material on and ultimately sculpted it into a shoulder to mirror Vincent's right shoulder. After the material hardened, the technician took it off and took it with him. It was the mold he would use to make the prosthetic shoulder.

After a couple of weeks, the prosthetic shoulder was ready and we went to the medical supply office so that Vincent could try it on to see if it needed modifications. It was brown to simulate the color of Vincent's skin and the prosthetic reached below his ribs on the left side with straps to connect on the right side of his chest to hold it in place. When he tried it on at the doctor's office, he was fine and the fit was perfect. Vincent was excited to have the prosthetic and he could not wait to wear it. Disappointedly, when he tried to wear it, especially to work, he noticed that the material of the prosthetic was not flexible. It restricted his movement and caused discomfort in his back. Thinking it would take some getting used to and that maybe he needed to break it in like a new pair of shoes, he still tried to wear it. Ultimately, he realized it was just too uncomfortable to work in but he did use it outside of work, especially when he went to church because his shirts and suit jackets fit much better when he wore the prosthetic shoulder.

For Vincent's 48th birthday, which was October 20, 2013, Vincent and I planned a birthday dinner at his favorite restaurant. Our children and grandchildren came over to celebrate his birthday before we went to dinner. We also went to his mom's house to celebrate with her and take a couple of pictures. If we were in town for his birthday, he made sure to go by and celebrate his birthday with his mom. She usually had a card, a big hug and a kiss for Vincent on his birthday. Vincent's brother Eric was also at her house, and he took pictures with him as well. At the restaurant, we were seated in a booth facing each other.

While sitting at dinner, I noticed the discomfort Vincent felt from wearing the prosthetic shoulder. I could see how it restricted him from moving as he normally would. He had to keep his back straight because the prosthetic went down past his ribs. I believe the prosthetic would've been better serving if the shoulder and top arm portion was made of a nonpliable material and the lower portion had been made from a pliable material so that it wasn't so restricting. Despite the discomfort, he still made the best of it and did not complain. Still wearing his big smile, we chit-chatted and laughed. He ordered his favorite ribeye steak and baked potato, and I had the chicken breast and vegetables. We both ordered a glass of wine to toast in celebration of the occasion. As we raised our glasses, I said, "Happy Birthday to the love of my life, the strongest, most amazing man I know. I look forward to the rest of our lives together. I love you," and we tapped our glasses together and took a sip of the wine. We enjoyed Vincent's birthday dinner, and we went home to continue the birthday celebration in private.

Chapter 17

Not Again

About a week or so after we celebrated Vincent's birthday, he informed me that something felt abnormal at the amputation site. "Lo, it feels like there is some fluid in here," he said while pointing to the site of the shoulder removal. When I placed my hand on the area, it was warm, but I could not feel what he was feeling.

"Maybe it's because the prosthetic is rubbing against the area and has caused some fluid to build up there," I said. I was hoping that was what he was feeling and not that the cancer had come back.

"I'm gonna call the doctor's office to let him know," he said. The following day, he called Dr. Shands' office and the nurse gave him an appointment to come in for a scan. The scan was normal, and the doctor gave him the all-clear as far as the scan was concerned. We returned home thinking all was well. I told the doctor the same thing I told Vincent, that the prosthetic rubbing against the area might have caused fluid to build up there. He said that it could have, but there was no sign of the cancer which was great news.

The following Sunday after leaving church, Vincent and I went to the hospital to visit the husband of a very dear family friend whom he called his second mother. She and Vincent's mom refer to one another as sisters. We had gone a couple of days before, but she wasn't there and her husband was sleeping. We left and decided to go back after church, hoping she would be there so we could visit with her as well. When we arrived at his hospital room, she was there along with some of her other family members. We embraced each other as we entered the room. Her husband was awake at the time and Vincent talked with him and encouraged him. We visited with them for about thirty minutes, which was a little long because her husband was in ICU. Vincent was happy that he was able to bring a smile to not only his second mother's face, but also to her husband's face. He had such a positive and enthusiastic attitude about life, and he was able to share it with those he felt needed encouragement and hope. After praying with the family, we embraced everyone and returned home.

Later that evening, we were watching television and Vincent said, "Lo, I feel a sharp pain in my chest." We had just finished eating dinner and were relaxing on the couch.

"Maybe it's gas," I said, and I told him to do what I usually do if I feel like I have gas: "Stretch and move around to see if you can get the gas to move." He started moving his right arm back and forth while kneeling on the floor facing the couch. "Does it feel like it's moving?" I asked.

"No, it's still there," he said.

"It can't be anything serious," I thought because a couple of days ago, we got the all-clear from the doctor. The cancer did not cross my mind at all, and I was certain it was not a heart attack so I wondered what else it could be. I monitored him throughout the evening and later I asked him, "Is the pain still there?"

"Not as bad, but it's still there," he responded.

After moving to our bedroom, we made love and went to sleep. The next morning, which was Monday, Vincent got up for work at 5:30 as he usually did. Trying to adjust my eyes to the light, I looked over at the bathroom where he was and saw him beckoning with his hand for me to come on and get up. I got out the bed and began helping him as I had been doing since his shoulder amputation. "How do you feel this morning?" I asked.

"I feel all right, but the pain is still there," he said. "

You still going to work?" I asked.

"Yeah, I'm alright," he responded. As usual, we began our morning routine: After he dressed for work, I pinned his shirt sleeve so the sleeve was on the inside of the shirt. Then he got his lunch out of the refrigerator and put it in his lunch carrier along with his phantom pain medication. He sat at the kitchen table to put his work boots on and I tied his shoestrings for him. I walked him to the door, kissed him and said, "Love you bae. Have a great day." But that morning, I felt some apprehension about him going to work because he still had that chest pain.

About an hour or so later, I received a phone call from Vincent's supervisor telling me that he was taking Vincent to the emergency room because he was coughing up a little blood. Immediately, I got dressed and met them at the hospital. After arriving at the hospital, I checked in with security to receive my identification sticker so I could go back to see Vincent. As I walked down the hall, I saw him sitting up in the bed in one of the rooms still fully dressed in his work clothes and work boots. His supervisor was with him and as I approached the room, his supervisor met me to tell me what he observed. He said Vincent told him he coughed up a little blood and that he had a pain in his chest. "Hey, bae," I said as I walked in the room and gave him a kiss. Then I asked, "How ya feeling?"

"I went to work and started coughing up a little blood. The doctor ordered some x-rays," he said.

The x-ray technician came in and took Vincent back to have x-rays done on his chest and he later returned him to the room. "You have a collapsed lung and we must get a chest tube inserted as soon as possible," the doctor said as he walked in the room.

"We need to get him to Shands Hospital in Gainesville," I interjected immediately because I knew that the local doctors and hospitals were not familiar with Vincent's health issues.

"He can't go anywhere until we get a chest tube in him," the emergency room physician said. "One lung is 90% collapsed and the other one is 10% collapsed. I don't even know how you went to work," he said to Vincent.

"If you only knew what else he did with a collapsed lung," I thought to myself because we had made love the night before. The doctor inserted a chest tube and Vincent was admitted to the hospital, but I was determined to take him to Shands where his doctor was. I contacted Dr. Shands' office in Gainesville and told his nurse what was going on with Vincent. They agreed that Vincent should come to Shands. Dr. Shands' nurse informed us that the doctor was out of town at a conference, but he had informed another lung specialist that Vincent was coming and he would take care of him when he got to the hospital. Dr. Shands' office was in touch with the hospital in Sanford and after spending two nights there, Vincent was transported by ambulance to Shands Hospital.

I followed the ambulance in my car. When we arrived at Shands, it was like the red carpet was rolled out for him. I do not know if Vincent felt the special treatment, but I sure did. They were waiting for him, and the lung specialist put Vincent in the ICU. They removed the chest tube Vincent had from the other hospital and replaced it with one of theirs. "Why is he in ICU?" I asked the doctor because in Sanford, he was in a regular room.

"Dr. Shands told me he was coming and to take good care of him," the doctor responded. "In ICU, I will have him under constant watch," he told me.

"Okay," I responded. I thought, "That makes sense because surely Vincent is not sick enough to be in ICU," so I was satisfied with the answer the doctor gave me. They even brought me a cot so that I could stay with him in the ICU. The ICU was not a private room, and the beds were not separated by walls; there was only a curtain that separated the patient's beds from each other. One night, a lady in the bed next to Vincent's bed died and we heard as the doctors and nurses tried and tried to keep her alive but to no avail. Her family members came, sat with her a while, and then left mourning their loss. Because Vincent's room was next to the door, they had to pass us to get to her bed. We saw when they came and as they left and let them know they had our sympathy.

The lung specialist informed us that the cancer had spread to Vincent's lungs. I thought, "Here we go again. Why wasn't the cancer detected by the scans that were taken a week earlier?" I also thought about Dr. Shands' statement: 'If the cancer spreads to the lungs, there is nothing more we could do for him.' After being there for a couple of days, the lung specialist said he needed to go in and repair Vincent's lungs. Vincent agreed to the surgery and it was scheduled. Before the surgery, Vincent and I agreed that after he came out of surgery, I would drive back to Sanford to get more clothes for me and return to Gainesville the following afternoon. Up until that time, I had slept in a cot in the ICU and I had not had a shower. I only had some quick morning wash ups in one of the public restrooms at the hospital, so I definitely needed to go home to take a shower. I was also looking forward to sleeping in my own bed. The morning of the surgery, the attendants came in and took Vincent to the surgery area while I went to the waiting room and waited for someone to come and inform me when the surgery was done.

After some hours, someone came to the waiting area and told me the surgery was over, Vincent was in recovery, and I would be able to see him shortly. When I went back to see him, he was still sleeping from the anesthesia so I did not wake him. I just stood over him, watched him, and began praising God for what He was doing. As the tears rolled down my face, I was praising and thanking God and the lung specialist walked in. He looked at me and asked, "How is he doing?"

"He's fine," I said, but I think he asked that because he saw my tears. Besides, he had to know how he was doing since he had just operated on him.

He went on to say, "One of his lungs was really bad; part of it was shredded like raw ground beef and I cut that part out and his other lung is also collapsed so we had to put in more chest tubes." Vincent went into surgery with one chest tube and he came out of surgery with four chest tubes: two on the left side in the upper and lower portion of the lung and two on the right side in the upper and lower portion. We had recorded Vincent in all the previous procedures he had done for the cancer, but it did not even enter my mind to bring the camcorder this time and I guess he did not think about it either because he did not mention it. But the four chest tubes are the one thing I regret not having in a picture. With the four chest tubes in, Vincent reminded me of the Spider Man nemesis in the movies with several arm-like appendages coming from his body.

The sun had already gone down, and it was getting late. Although we had agreed that I would leave after the surgery, I did not want to leave Vincent because I believed I needed to be there with him. Vincent began to wake up and we talked a little; I told him I did not want to leave him. "Lo, it's getting late; if you're going, you need to go ahead and leave because I don't want you on the road too late. I will be fine, and I will see you tomorrow," he said.

"I know, I know, I'm leaving," I said. I was a little frustrated with him telling me I needed to go ahead and leave because it seemed as if he was rushing me to leave, but I knew it was because of his concern for me being on the road alone after dark with a two-hour drive. He also told me to make sure I call the hospital when I arrived home to let him know I had made it home safely. We said our goodbyes, I gave him a kiss, left the hospital and headed back to Sanford. I tried to call the hospital to let him know I had made it home but he did not get the message, which was fine because he most likely slept through the night from the anesthesia.

Vincent Jr. was at the house when I arrived home, and I walked in and gave him a big hug. Although the doctor said he removed the damaged part of the lung in the surgery, during the drive home, I thought again about Dr. Shands saying that if the cancer spread to the lungs, Vincent would probably die. I wanted to fall into Vincent Jr.'s arms and cry because unlike dealing with the cancer in the past where I had an unshakable confidence that Vincent would be fine, this time it was different. I did not have that certainty. That was the first time my heart felt heavy about Vincent's illness, and I wanted someone to assure me that he would be fine; but I didn't want to put that on Vincent Jr., so I did not say anything to him about my feelings. This was not the same feeling I had when Vincent had the shoulder amputation because although my spirit was in turmoil because I did not understand why God let him go so far as to have his shoulder amputated, the possibility of his death did not have to be considered at that time.

"How's Da doing?" Vincent Jr. asked.

"The surgery went well," I said.

"Good," he replied. I told him about the four chest tubes his father had and why he had them. I wanted to relax when I got home but I couldn't. I began washing clothes and doing a little cleaning around the house. Since I could not be where I wanted to be, which was at the hospital with Vincent, I had to keep myself busy doing something. My bags were ready before I lay down for bed that night so I could leave early the following morning. I am sure the hot shower and my bed was something I needed but because of the urgency I felt to get back to the hospital to Vincent, I did not get the soothing encounter I wanted.

When I returned to the hospital the following day, I went up to see Vincent and he was in a different ICU room. Unlike the previous one, this ICU room was private. There was also a chair in the room that let out into a bed so again, I was able to sleep in the room with him. The room was a bit of a graduation from the first ICU as far as his health was concerned. He still had the four chest tubes, and the doctor informed me that he would have the chest tubes until the air holes in his lungs closed, but Vincent was fully alert and his normal strong self.

The first morning at about 5am, the technicians came in with their x-ray machine to get x-rays. I was awakened out of a deep sleep to let me know I had to step out of the room while they took the x-rays. Somewhat disoriented I stepped out of the room into the hallway until they were done. The next morning, they did the same thing and after a couple of mornings of them coming in, I finally realized that they had to get an x-ray each morning, so I prepared my mind to know that they were coming in each morning around the same time and that I had to be ready to leave the room.

One problem Vincent had this time that he did not have before was he had to take the four chest tubes with him when he used the bedside commode, and each tube had a separate box. I became quite efficient at keeping the chest tubes and the boxes separated while moving them over near the commode when he used it because if each chest tube along with the connecting box was not kept separated from the other ones, the chest tubes became a twisted mess. Each time he said, "Lo, I gotta pee," I had to assist him with those tubes so he could get to the bedside commode. It was on the right side of his bed, so I grabbed the two tubes with the boxes on the left side, keeping one separate from the other and brought them around to the right side of the bed and sat them on the floor by the commode. Then I grabbed the two tubes on the right side as he got out of bed and sat them on the floor on the right side of the commode on the floor.

When the nurses walked in the room and saw the four chest tubes, they looked as if they had not seen anything like that before. Also, when Vincent had to leave the room for tests, the nurses came in to help move his chest tubes but they made it more difficult than it was. Vincent was trying to instruct the nurses as to how to move the chest tubes along with the boxes, but they were not listening to him and his patience ran out with them. "Lo, come show them how to move these chest tubes," Vincent said as he beckoned to me with his hand.

"I am not about to tell them nurses how to do their job," I said. "They will figure it out," and they did. It took them a little while, but they did.

After a couple of weeks, both chest tubes on the right side were taken out and one on the bottom left side was taken out, so Vincent had one that remained on the upper left side. That last chest tube was the hold up from Vincent being released from the hospital. One of the doctors came in to talk to us and she said it looked like they got the cancer during the surgery, but they wanted to do a procedure to make sure his lungs did not collapse again. The procedure, called pleurodesis, adheres the lung to the wall of the chest to prevent it from collapsing. They explained to us that it was an irritant drug placed in the space so that the lung would stick to the chest wall. After receiving light anesthesia, Vincent was placed in a bed that vibrated aggressively, so that the irritant would reach every part of his chest. When the procedure was completed, I went to see Vincent and he said, "Lo, they left me in here all by myself; I was trying to yell for help, but I couldn't yell, and nobody came." When the nurse came back into the room, I told her what he said.

"I was in there with him the whole time; he wasn't alone," she said. "Hi, Mr. Paige," she said to Vincent.

"Why didn't you come help me?" he asked softly still feeling the effects of the anesthesia.

"I never left you, Mr. Paige, I was with you the whole time," she answered. It must have been the anesthesia that caused him to think he was alone.

With Thanksgiving fast approaching, Vincent was out of the ICU and in a regular room. We were hoping that he would be released from the hospital by Thanksgiving, but that did not happen. I wanted to be home because we enjoyed cooking Thanksgiving dinner together for our family; well, I cooked, and he helped by chopping the vegetables and herbs. He was also my food-taster. The hospital staff said they were bringing in dishes for Thanksgiving and that we were welcome to have some. It was a nice gesture but I did not know them well enough to eat their food, so I told Vincent I was going home the Wednesday before Thanksgiving to cook our dinner and I would return on Thanksgiving Day with a meal that I knew we would both enjoy. "My wife is going home to cook me a Thanksgiving meal," he happily told the staff when they mentioned the Thanksgiving dinner they were having at the hospital.

The Wednesday before Thanksgiving, I left the hospital early in the afternoon to make the two-hour trip back to Sanford. When I arrived in Sanford, I went to the grocery store to get what I needed for Thanksgiving dinner. As soon as I arrived home, I started cooking the cake and sweet potato pie, chopped the vegetables for the stuffing and seasoned the turkey to put in the oven later that night. I woke up early the following morning and finished cooking our dinner. I called the kids to let them know I had cooked and that they were welcome to get something to eat, but I had to get back to the hospital. After fixing Vincent and I a plate, I left to go back to Gainesville, and we ate and enjoyed our Thanksgiving dinner. The children and grandchildren came to the hospital that weekend as they had done since the time Vincent had been in the hospital.

Dr. Shands came to the hospital to visit Vincent and he jokingly said, "I've never seen you with an afro," because Vincent had not had a hair cut in a while. Vincent was bald on top with hair growing on the sides, so I didn't see an afro, but that's what the doctor called it. "I'm sorry I wasn't here when you came in; I had to go to a conference," he said. After all the cordialities, he asked, "You know what this means don't you?" He was referring to what he told us that if the cancer spreads to the lungs, Vincent would probably die.

"Yes, but I still trust God to do what He wills to do," Vincent answered.

"I have never had a patient with your attitude. I have patients that would've been throwing f-bombs if this had happened to them. I am going to speak about you in my conferences," he said.

The entire time Vincent was in the hospital, I was in contact with Victor to keep him informed of what was going on. One day, Victor called me to see how Vincent was doing but I had left the hospital for a short while to eat lunch at one of the restaurants nearby while Vincent was having a medical procedure done. Victor did not like that I was alone at the hospital with Vincent. "I'm coming," he said.

"You don't have to come now, Victor, we're fine and I might need you to come later," I said. However, I could not talk him out of coming and Thanksgiving evening, Victor arrived in Sanford and came to Gainesville the following day with our son Vincent Jr. I am so thankful Victor came because him being there encouraged me and Vincent. By this time, Vincent was out of the ICU and in a regular room. The hospital supplied a pull-out bed in Vincent's room for me to sleep in. Victor stayed in a hotel a couple of nights until the hospital gave him a reclining chair in the room to sleep in, so we both stayed at the hospital with Vincent. He stayed in Gainesville with us until Vincent was released from the hospital.

Vincent was released from the hospital shortly after Thanksgiving and he lost the weight he gained after his shoulder amputation. After he was released from the hospital, Vincent Jr. invited his dad's brothers and sisters to the house for breakfast and he and Victor cooked the food. We had grits, eggs, Italian sausage, orange juice and coffee. We ate, talked, laughed and took pictures. Vincent was released from the hospital with one chest tube still in because one air hole did not close completely. The chest tube was attached to a small plastic air bag that Vincent wore strapped to his lower leg. When the bag filled with air, the air had to be released. This had to be done several times a day at first but as the hole closed, the bag did not fill as fast. Vincent showed our grandbabies how to release the air, and they eagerly helped their granddad. After several trips back to Gainesville to see if the chest tube was ready to come out, we finally got the "okay" for the removal of the chest tube and the doctor said his lungs looked much better. Removing the final chest tube helped to ease some of the heaviness I was feeling in my heart, and I was hoping Vincent would continue to feel better and defy the prognosis from the doctor of probable death.

After the chest tube was removed and while Victor was still in the states, Vincent made an appointment to see the doctor in Orlando and he referred Vincent to a lung specialist. After meeting with the lung specialist, Vincent was given the green light to do everything he wanted to do. The specialist said he had a patient whose diagnosis was parallel to Vincent's and the patient had returned to the physical activities he enjoyed, especially swimming. Victor went with us to see the specialist and he was pleased to hear that Vincent's lungs were looking good and that he could return to doing the physical activities he enjoyed, because he was leaving soon to go back to Turkey. The news eased his concerns about having to leave Vincent to return to Turkey.

Chapter 18

Back with a Vengeance

We didn't have much of a Christmas holiday with lights and decorations, nor did we buy any Christmas gifts. Our Christmas gift was that Vincent was home from the hospital and doing well; that was the best Christmas gift. My sister Gail was born on December 25th and that year, she was celebrating her 50th birthday. To continue in the family tradition of a 50th birthday party, we assisted her daughters, Tahesia, China, Curynn, and Briana, and gave her a party on the Friday after her birthday. It was an all-white party as they requested that everyone wear white attire. They also rented a venue for Gail's party and earlier in the day, we decorated it. Later that evening while getting dressed for the party, Vincent said, "Lo, don't expect me to dance tonight because I can't dance like I used to." It had been about a month since Vincent was released from the hospital, and he thought he would not be able to dance the way he used to dance before his lungs were compromised.

"Okay, we don't have to dance," I said. I guess with all the busyness of assisting with decorating the venue and rushing to get home and get ready for the party, I had not given his health issues or dancing at the party much thought. I was just happy that he was well enough to attend the party with me. Both of us enjoyed dancing, but since he had surgery about a month earlier, my guess is that he wanted to give me the heads up just in case he was not able to dance, which was understandable. He knew that dancing was one of our favorite activities and as soon as I heard the music, I would have wanted to dance and most likely would not have thought about his health issues so he put me on notice.

When we arrived at the party, I pitched in to help Gail's daughter with some last-minute preparations. The venue had a room upstairs and one downstairs and we utilized both rooms for the party. The dinner was served upstairs, and the music and dancing were downstairs. The white attire along with the crispness in the air were a perfect pair for the holiday season. The guests started arriving along with my mom, siblings, and other family members to make this 50th birthday party a memorable one. While waiting for the arrival of the guest of honor, we had a time of greeting the guests and talking with those we had not seen for a while. Then the time came for the guest of honor to enter the room escorted by one of her close friends. With her hair flowing around her shoulders, Gail walked in wearing a beautiful black dress which made her the only one at the party dressed in black so there was no mistaking who the guest of honor was. Her daughters asked me to emcee the party and they had given me a program to follow. Each one of them delivered words to celebrate their mom for her birthday. Then other family members and friends were allowed to speak as well.

When my turn came to speak, I told my son Delrick, who was the DJ, to play the song "December, 1963 (Oh, What a Night)." These are some of the words to that song: "Oh what a night in late December back in '63, what a very special time for me, what a lady, what a night." I don't know which lady the songwriter was speaking of, but it caused me to think about my sister. As the song played, the guests clapped their hands as the DJ let it play for about a minute. Afterwards, I started speaking, "Gail, I don't know if you remember this, but I bought that song when we were younger because late December of 1963 is the time of year that you were born; so when I heard it, I thought of you," and she acknowledged smiling. Also, I told her I felt she got slighted on her birthday because she had to share with Christmas. "Merry Christmas," we'd say excitedly, then "oh, and happy birthday Gail," is usually how her birthday went like it was an afterthought.

Then Vincent came up to speak and he began to say, "Gail, I want to thank you because you helped put me and my wife together." I'm sure he said happy birthday and some other things, but I remember him thanking her for putting us together because it was Gail who encouraged me to talk to him.

After the speakers, dinner was served; and after dinner, the party moved downstairs for music and dancing. Gail had given the DJ a list of songs she wanted him to play, and the music started playing. Vincent and I sat at a table with friends and family members. The music was playing and I wanted to dance but not without my husband. Then the DJ played one of the line dance songs and people were on the dance floor. Because I did not need a partner for a line dance song, I got up to dance. Then Vincent got up too and we both began dancing. He must have forgotten what he told me because we danced all night. I had gone upstairs to help with the cleanup and I heard him calling me from downstairs. "Lo," he yelled.

"Yeah, bae," I answered.

"Come on," he yelled to me. I leaned over the stairs to hear what was playing and it was an old school dance song, so I ran downstairs to dance with him. Once he started dancing, he did not want to sit down. We had a ball and if he was feeling any effects of what he had just endured with the cancer, he showed no signs of it at the party.

When we returned home, it was a different story. Vincent could not sleep because of the pain in his lower left side. I had never seen him in so much pain; the pain was relentless. Standing bent over a little with his right arm against the wall he said, "Lo, I need to go to the emergency room."

"The pain's that bad?" I asked.

"Yes," he responded. We went to the emergency room and after an examination, the emergency room physician prescribed something for the pain. Then, Vincent was released to go home. After returning home, the pain began to subside and Vincent was finally able to get some sleep. When he woke the following morning, he felt fine and did not have any more pain, so we ascribed the pain to him overdoing it at the party the night before.

Sunday morning, we went to church and told one of the members about the good time we had at Gail's party. "Did y'all dance?" she asked.

"Did we?" I responded. "All night long but we paid for it because Vincent was in so much pain, we were in the emergency room that night."

"It was all worth it though because I did what I enjoy doing," Vincent said.

In the latter part of the next month, which was January, the doctor released Vincent so he could return to work. "Bae, you sure you ready to go back?" I asked.

"I feel fine, Lo, and I want to go back to work," he said. I was not as certain as he was that he was ready to return to work, but I felt somewhat comforted because it was apparent that he had regained his strength and there were no visible signs of cancer. Vincent had started going to the gym again and we got back on the tennis court. Doing the activities that he enjoyed was just what the doctor ordered, and he was feeling great.

With Valentine's Day approaching, Vincent and I planned to go to his favorite restaurant for dinner. Because of past experiences on Valentine's Day of extra-long waits for a table at a restaurant even with a reservation, we went to dinner on February 13th to celebrate. Casually dressed, Vincent and I went to the restaurant.

Vincent wore some starched creased jeans, a long sleeve, button down, white collared shirt with baby blue and pink stripes, shirt tail hanging outside of his jeans and a pair of brown Timberland boots. Whatever his attire was, jeans with boots, or slacks with nice hard bottom shoes, he made the look distinguished. While at the restaurant, we ran into a family friend who was out with his family and after cordialities with them we were seated for dinner and enjoyed our pre-Valentine's Day evening.

Meanwhile, our granddaughters had been telling us they wanted to go to a hotel and the Saturday following Valentine's Day was the date we reserved. Going to hotels excited them so when we told them we were going, that was like Christmas for them, even if the hotel was just around the corner from their home. We were equally excited. All they cared about was being at the hotel. I reserved a room at the hotel on one of the websites that you choose by the area and star rating at a discounted price, but the name of the hotel is not known until after the reservation is made. Well, our reservation was with the Westin, which is a nice hotel, and it was fairly new in the area. After checking into the hotel and getting settled in, we decided to walk across the street to Dexter's to have lunch with our grands. Vincent walked behind and I noticed him cough and spit on the ground. I looked in the spit and I saw blood. As I looked up at him, our eyes met but we said nothing because we did not want to alarm our grands, so we continued walking. We both knew that him coughing up blood was not a good sign.

It was such a beautiful day, so we chose to have lunch outside. Spending time with our granddaughters was precious to us and we treasured those times. We sat, talked, laughed, and ate. After lunch, we walked to the Publix up the street and the girls picked out snacks to take back to the hotel room. Our plan was to return to the hotel, go to the pool for a while and afterwards, go to the room and play games. "How ya feeling bae?" I asked Vincent when we got back to the hotel.

"Oh, I'm fine," he responded with extra assurance to take away any concerns I had about him and temporarily, it did. Also, our attention was to our granddaughters and enjoying them, so I did not dwell on his health at that time.

When we returned to the hotel room, Vincent and our oldest granddaughter Lauryn took a nap, so they changed our plans. Me and our other two grands watched tv, waiting for them to wake up so we could go to the pool. Vincent woke up after a while, but Lauryn would not wake up. We tried to wake her up but with no success. She raised her head to look up with her heavy eyes and then laid her head back on the pillow and continued her sleep. She slept the entire evening and did not wake up until the following morning. Well so much for going to the pool, but Vincent and I played games and ate snacks with our other grands. When Lauryn finally woke up the next morning, her sisters tore into her to let her know that she was the reason they did not go to the pool because she would not wake up. Lauryn held her hands out and shrugged her shoulders as if to say, "Oh well." It was not surprising that Lauryn took a nap after our lunch because we all knew that Lauryn enjoyed eating and sleeping, but we did not think she would sleep all day. We did not spend time at the pool, but we had a relaxing enjoyable stay at the hotel and after checking out, we took the grands to breakfast and then headed home.

Vincent made an appointment to see Dr. Anderson after seeing the blood in his spit. The doctor ordered Vincent to have an MRI and after seeing the results, he said, "The cancer has come back and you have stage 4 lung cancer. We can try another round of chemo if you want to see if it will shrink the tumors."

"Okay, let's do the chemo," Vincent said calmly. From the calm tone of his voice, you would never have guessed that Vincent had just received the news that he had stage 4 lung cancer. The doctor scheduled three weeks of chemo for five days a week. Vincent was still working at the time, so the chemo was scheduled in the afternoon after work. It was much different this time because for his previous chemo, he was admitted to the hospital. This time, he checked in for the chemo and he went to a room where there were about eight chairs for the patients to sit in as they were taking the chemo. Rushing in from his job, Vincent came in the house, took a quick shower and then we headed to Orlando so he could take the chemo. After doing it for two weeks, Vincent requested another scan to see if the chemo was effective in shrinking the tumors. "Lo, I don't want to do this if it is not helping me," he said. The scan showed that the tumor was not shrinking so Vincent refused the remaining week of chemo.

Vincent and I began noticing more tumors in different areas of his body. Not only did one appear at the amputation site, but he noticed one on his lower left side and I noticed one on his butt as I rubbed his body while we were making love. Initially, I did not say anything because I did not want it to be a tumor. But later I said, "Vincent, I felt a growth on your butt when I was rubbing it." I was hoping it was not the cancer spreading.

Then he said, "I feel one on my side too, Lo." It seemed like the cancer had come back with a vengeance and was consuming the chemo drugs for its food. At the next doctor's appointment, we told the doctor about the tumors we noticed.

"Yeah, the chemo is not working and you're dying," he said bluntly. He went on to say, "It could be two weeks, six months, we don't know; but I want you to consider calling hospice." Vincent was still working and he said he felt fine, so I was just not receiving what the doctor said about my husband dying and that we needed to call the hospice because that meant death. In my eyes, Vincent was nowhere near death. He was so strong and full of vigor. In fact, we were still playing tennis. Every now and then after a point, he had to stop and lean on his tennis racquet to catch his breath, but he ran the balls down and hit them just as he had always done. The doctor had to be wrong.

We left the doctor's office and stopped at Firehouse Subs to get us a bite to eat. When we walked in the door, we saw our pastor sitting at the counter eating. After speaking, I said, "Vincent, you can tell him what the doctor said and I will go order our subs," so Vincent sat and talked with him while I ordered the subs. I went back to talk with them while our subs were being prepared. "I understand the gravity of what is going on, but I can't live in it," I said to my pastor as Vincent told him what the doctor said. If I had dwelled on the thought of Vincent's impending death or what the doctor had said, I would have been a wreck. Vincent did not have a problem talking about the doctor's prognosis of death for him. I, on the other hand, did not care to discuss it with anyone, not even my family members. I did not want to hear the clichés such as "trust God," "just have faith," or any of the other religious sayings people say.

Our pastor's response was not any of those statements. He simply said, "Really?" with a bewildered look on his face because looking at Vincent, seeing his vigor and strength, you would not have thought that death from cancer could be only months or maybe weeks away.

When we got home, we told the children what the doctor said but they knew our trust was in God and not in what the doctors said. Vincent called his mom and siblings to inform them of what the doctor said. I could not speak with my mom or siblings about it. I wanted them to be informed, but I did not want to be the one to have to do it. "You have to tell Mama, Vincent, because I can't do it," I said to him.

"Okay," he said, and we went to my mama's house so he could tell her what the doctor said. "But I feel fine, Ms. Helen, and I am still trusting God," he said when he finished. He talked about it like he was talking about someone else, as if it was not happening to him.

Vincent and I were riding in the car one day and he asked, "Lo, what will you do if I die?" I knew he thought about it, but he had never asked me what I thought about it.

"I don't know, Vincent. I try not to think about it, but I wonder why God would give us *this* and then take it from us," I said.

"I know," he said. The *this* I was referring to was what God had given us in our marriage. God gave us a marriage that we never dreamed we could have because we had never seen a marriage like ours. I know that sounds either naïve or conceited on my part because surely there have been and will be some great marriages, but we had never been in the company of one like ours. For God to take us from where we started to where we were in our marriage was nothing short of miraculous.

Chapter 19

Hospice Called

God had done so many wonderful works in our lives and in our marriage, and I was not ready to concede to the thought of not having my husband anymore. That's why hospice was immediately refused by me. "Vincent, you don't need hospice," I said. The only other experience I had with hospice was with my brother Tony. When my sister-in-law called hospice for my brother, I did not want to accept that he was dying but it was not unreasonable. Tony's health had been failing for a while and when hospice was called, he was not doing much eating or drinking. He did not even have the strength to walk or do anything for himself, so calling hospice was understandable. But Vincent was still working and doing everything for himself so to me, it was too soon for hospice to come out. He did not seem close to dying to me.

Vincent did not call hospice, the doctor's office did. They gave hospice Vincent's contact information and asked them to call him, and they did. When Vincent received the call, he scheduled an appointment for a representative from hospice to come to the house. The hospice representative was pleasant, and she informed Vincent of the services they offered. Vincent thanked her for coming to the house, but he informed her that he did not need the services at that time and that he would call should he see the need to. The one thing he did do was sign a do not resuscitate (DNR) form that the hospice representative provided.

All the talk of Vincent dying and calling hospice began to weigh heavily on me. One day I saw myself waving a white flag in surrender as I cried out to God and said, "God, I thought I could do this, but I can't do this!" I was still in denial of the possibility that my husband's illness might end in death. There was no way God was going to allow this sickness to end Vincent's life. When Vincent came in from work that day, I said to him still crying, "Vincent, I can't do this; it's too much for me." I did not know what 'this' was but whatever God had us going through, I did not think I could do it, especially if it meant the death of my husband.

Vincent continued working for a couple of weeks after the hospice representative came out, but he soon found it difficult to walk up the stairs at work. He told me one of his coworkers saw him laboring to go upstairs and she said, "I see you had to stop when you reached the top to catch your breath. Are you sure you can still do this?" she asked him.

When he came home from work, he said, "Lo, today I took another medical leave from work. It's becoming too difficult to go up and down the stairs." He had informed his supervisor at his job of all that the doctor had said, even of hospice coming out to the house, so they did not have a problem with him taking another medical leave. They were more than supportive of Vincent during his sickness and approved the medical leaves when he needed them. That was the last medical leave he had to take because that day, March 19, 2014, was his last day of employment.

Vincent's health began to rapidly deteriorate but we were still attending church services together. After service the following Sunday, I asked a couple of the elders in the church to help me fight for my husband's life because I was watching what cancer was doing to him and it looked like cancer was winning. One of the elders walked out to the car with me because Vincent went immediately to the car after service. "Man, keep the faith and I am fighting with you," he said.

"I have faith and whatever God's will is, I'm fine with it," Vincent said calmly. One of the other elders told me he was praying and fasting for Vincent. That afternoon, Vincent and I went downtown to walk along the river front, which is something we often did on Sunday afternoons. We began walking and I noticed Vincent was particularly weak. He walked at a much slower pace than usual. The previous Sunday when we walked, he was fine. It was perplexing to me because I did not notice the weakness before we began to take our walk. I am not sure if it was my denial, or the fact that we had not gone anywhere that he had to walk at a decent pace.

"Bae, are you alright?" I asked.

"I just feel really weak," he said. Because of how he was feeling, we cut our walk short and returned home.

As we sat in our bedroom talking, I started crying and I said, "Vincent I can't do this." He grabbed me with a strong embrace and started praying for me, and I started praying too. Both of us were crying and praying. Then after a few minutes, he called our pastor and asked him to pray for me that I would be able to accept what God was doing. Vincent did not ask him to pray for him but for me. He was not concerned about himself; he was concerned about me. Our pastor began to pray while we were still crying and praying. After we finished praying, our pastor began talking to us and encouraging us.

Vincent seemed to be fine if he did not have to walk at a decent pace or distance. However, the following Friday morning, he woke feeling exceptionally weak and wanted to go to the hospital. In fact, because of his weakness, he needed my help getting dressed, which had not happened until that moment. He also wanted to go to the hospital in Orlando since that hospital had all the medical records concerning the cancer. After sitting for hours in the emergency room, he was finally seen by the ER doctor and was told that his hemoglobin was low and that was why he was weak. They admitted him to the hospital to give him a blood transfusion to get his hemoglobin up. After the blood transfusion and spending two nights in the hospital, the doctor discharged him to go home. Vincent had called his twin brother in Turkey and told him what happened with the low hemoglobin and his hospital stay. Victor caught the next flight from Turkey to be here with Vincent and he arrived in the states on Monday, March 30th. We never followed up with Dr. Anderson to let him know Vincent had been in the hospital because of low hemoglobin and he felt much better after the transfusion, so he did not see a need to call him. However, the doctor saw the need to call Vincent and scheduled an appointment for him to come in.

We arrived at the doctor's office and he walked in and said, "I see where you came into the emergency room and you needed a blood transfusion because your hemoglobin was low."

"Yes, I felt weak and they said that was the reason for it," Vincent responded.

"How did you get up here?" he asked referring to his office.

"I walked up," Vincent responded.

"Did you walk from the parking garage?" the doctor asked while he gave Vincent the trash can to spit in.

"Yes," Vincent answered.

The doctor shook his head in amazement because he did not understand how Vincent had the strength to walk to his office unassisted. We walked from the parking garage of the hospital and across the street to MD Anderson to get to the doctor's office, which was a good distance to walk. While sitting and talking with the doctor, Vincent coughed and blood came up in his spit. The doctor said, "Yeah, don't come back to the hospital. Call hospice because you're dying." Vincent shook his head in agreement, and I was getting pissed.

"But we're still believing God," I said.

"Oh, sure," the doctor responded but all I heard him heartlessly say was, 'Stay home and die.' I thought to myself, "Listen to the ego of this man; because he could not do anymore for my husband, he told him to stay home and die; how arrogant."

The more I thought about what had happened in the doctor's office, the more pissed I became. "Vincent, he called you in to see him to tell you not to come back to the hospital because he couldn't do nothing else for you," I said in disgust. I could not believe he called Vincent into his office to tell him not to come back.

The doctor didn't show any empathy for Vincent, but Vincent had empathy for him because he calmly said, "Lo, he's just doing what they are supposed to do." Vincent was weak and not feeling well. I believed he was vulnerable and could not fight for himself, so I thought I had to fight for him. Where was the personable doctor we initially met who talked about his enjoyment of playing basketball because he knew my husband enjoyed playing, even to the point of inviting my husband and our sons to a gym in Orlando to play with him and some of his friends? Where was the doctor who talked about his love of going on cruises with his wife when he learned that my husband and I enjoyed going on cruises as well? And where were the bedside manners that doctors are supposed to have? When he told my husband not to come back, the pleasantness he showered us with went out the window and the only thing left for me about him was disgust. Why did he make it a pretense to get personable with my husband as if he cared about him as a person and not just as a patient?

Vincent stopped by his place of employment after we left the doctor's office. "Lo, I want to go say bye to everybody," he said. As I watched Vincent slowly walk up the steps to his job, the thought 'walking tall' came to me because that is what he was doing. He was not feeling well, his strength was diminished, and he had just received word from the doctor that he was dying, but he still wanted to personally say goodbye to his Invacare family. While I sat in the car and waited, I cried and I prayed, because the heaviness I felt in my spirit would not go away. About twenty minutes later, Vincent came back to the car with papers in his hands. "Lo, if anything happens to me, this is how much you will get," he said.

"I don't wanna know how much I'll get if you die," I said. I did not want to hear that, because I did not want to think about him dying.

"No, Lo, you have to know this," he said, so I took the papers because he wanted me to but I didn't look at them. "I talked to everyone in the front office and told them I won't be coming back. I told them I was thankful for my Invacare family and that I enjoyed working with them," he said. "I wanted to walk out on the floor, but I didn't have the strength, so I called certain ones to the office to tell them goodbye."

After leaving Vincent's job, we went home and I was still pissed and disgusted by Dr. Anderson's actions from earlier that day. I called Fantasy to tell her and before I could get three words out of my mouth, I was sobbing. "You want me to come over there?" she asked.

"Yeah," I responded. Before she arrived, Victor, Vincent and I were sitting in the living room talking about what the doctor had said.

"Are y'all alright?" Victor asked.

"No, I'm not alright," I said. "Vincent, I can't watch you die," I said crying. Vincent did not say anything, but he looked at me as if he understood me but could not do anything about it. No matter what the doctors said, I was not ready to give up my belief that God was going to cure Vincent of the cancer and not let him die. I thought I had relinquished my will to God, but I had not. I was still holding on to what I wanted and the anger that I was feeling wasn't because of what the doctor did or did not do, it was because of what God was not doing. Vincent's death seemed inevitable and my heart was breaking because my hope was that God would heal him; but it was becoming more and more apparent that was not going to happen.

Fantasy finally made it to the house and after asking her dad how he was doing, she and I went outside and talked. "Are you alright?" she asked.

"I am better now," I said. I told her what had happened at the doctor's office and how disgusted I was with what I perceived as his arrogance.

April 1st was our nineteenth wedding anniversary. It was always a time of celebration for me and Vincent but this year, I was not expecting anything because of my husband's illness. Vincent and Victor had gone out together earlier in the day. I was home when I heard a knock at the door, and it was the flower delivery person with a vase of beautiful red roses. No matter how much I told Vincent that he did not have to get me flowers, he loved sending them to me. It did not have to be a special occasion such as our anniversary; he did it just because. However, that day it was particularly special for me to receive those roses from my husband. He had every excuse in the world not to do anything for our anniversary; but that let me know that he was not doing it because I expected him to do it, but because he wanted to do it. The card inside said, "Happy Anniversary, My Princess, I Love You." Then he came home and walked into the house with that big grin he wears when he does things to let me know how much he loves me. It made him happy when he saw me happy.

Some of our family came over because they wanted to celebrate our anniversary with us and see Vincent. I was still in protection mode and did not want much company because I did not want anyone to come around my husband with the negative talk or behavior of someone dying. "Vincent, I don't want nobody coming over here waiting on you to die," I said, because he was still full of life. Because of my breaking heart, I might have been a little unreasonable but my husband was not dead, and I did not want the mood of death around him. After sitting and talking with them for a little, Vincent and I left them inside and we took a walk around our apartment complex. The family members did not stay long and after they left, we were sitting around the house and one of our favorite songs came on the radio: "Let's Get Married" (the remix) by Jagged Edge. Vincent got up and started dancing as if there was nothing wrong with him, with energy, his dancing facial expressions and all. Looking at him in awe, I asked, "Is that what we need to do? Go dancing?" I had not seen that energy in him in weeks.

"Alright now, don't get carried away," he said smiling letting me know that was only for a minute.

That evening, Vincent and I went to our favorite restaurant. We ordered carryout because he did not feel up to dining in the restaurant. After picking up our dinner, we returned home to eat. Excitedly, I sat at the dining table to enjoy some good food with my husband on our anniversary and Vincent said, "I don't know what it is, but it just don't taste like it usually does." I so wanted Vincent to eat and enjoy dinner, because I wanted to see that he still had the strength to eat a hearty meal, but he did not. I did not enjoy my dinner either. The taste of it was not what I expected, and I believed the restaurant did not prepare our food properly. We were disappointed with our meals and I made sure to send a long email to the company to let them know of our disappointment. I informed them that we were celebrating our anniversary and that we ordered our meals to go. However, we were both dissatisfied with the taste of our food. They were very apologetic and sent gift cards in the mail to compensate us for our food and experience. Initially, I blamed the restaurant for us not enjoying our meal; but the more I thought about it, the restaurant wasn't to blame.

Vincent did not enjoy his meal because of the cancer, and I did not enjoy my meal because he didn't enjoy his.

Throughout that week, Vincent continued to spend time with Victor. They spent time visiting with family and friends since Vincent was not working and he was still feeling well enough to drive. Then towards the end of the week, Vincent started feeling ill again and he was running a fever. Remembering what Dr. Anderson told him about not coming back to the hospital, he called hospice and a nurse came to the house. After checking Vincent over, she wanted him to go to a hospital that hospice used that was a little distance from our apartment. "I'm not going down there; I'm going right here in Sanford where my doctor is," Vincent said. He was still in communication with his primary care doctor and he never turned Vincent away. I took Vincent to the emergency room in Sanford and after checking him over, they said he had pneumonia and admitted him to the hospital. Victor stayed with him each night while he was in the hospital. The doctor prescribed medicine to treat the pneumonia and while he was in the hospital, his primary doctor came to see him daily along with a cancer doctor from the area. After a few days of receiving treatment for the pneumonia, Vincent was feeling much better and was discharged to go home.

The same hospice nurse who wanted him to go to the hospital they were affiliated with came to see Vincent a couple of days later. We sat at our dining table to discuss what she thought Vincent should do regarding his illness. During the discussion, Vincent's friend Victor from Atlanta came to the apartment to see how he was doing. Victor and Vincent became friends while Vincent was working at Invacare. The company Victor worked for did business with Invacare and through them having to communicate with each other, they became friends. They not only talked regarding the business of the job but they also shared the common faith in Christ Jesus, and they talked about that as well. Although Vincent and I were talking with the hospice nurse, we still welcomed Victor into our apartment because Vincent was so delighted to see him. There was no way we were going to tell him we were busy and to come back later, so we told him to have a seat. He sat in the living room but he could hear what we were discussing with the hospice nurse.

We informed her that Vincent was admitted to the hospital with pneumonia. "What are you going to do next time it happens? It's like plugging a leak in a hose but you know another leak is coming somewhere else. You just can't keep plugging the holes up," she said.

Now here she was pissing me off too. "You know what, you sound just like the cancer doctor. I didn't like what he said and I don't like what you're saying either, and I want you to leave. That's the same stuff the doctor was saying and you sound just like him," I said to her. I don't think she expected me to respond in that way because she looked puzzled, but I meant what I said.

At first Vincent did not say much, but then he took control of the situation. "Wait a minute," he said. "I know my body and I will know when it's time for y'all to do what you need to do. Until then, I will go to the hospital to get treatment when I need it." After Vincent said what he said, I calmed down and apologized to the nurse. I went on to tell her what Dr. Anderson had told Vincent.

"Oh no, I understand," she said. "This is your husband and you are fighting for him." The only thing she did was tell me the truth but I could not handle the truth, so I got angry with her. I could not bear the thought of him dying and I did not want to hear talk of it. When Victor heard and saw what was happening, he called Vincent Jr. out of his bedroom and said, "Come ride off with me," and they left the apartment.

Vincent and I continued talking after the nurse left. "Vincent, I'm sorry, but I don't like the way they talk; they don't give you no hope," I said.

"Lo, I'm not looking to them for hope; the Lord is my hope," he said, and I agreed with him. God was my hope too but I was hoping for God to heal him, and it did not look like that was going to happen.

Then I jokingly said, "Don't she know we had relations last night," like the grandma said in the movie The Nutty Professor.

The previous night, Vincent and I were lying in bed and he said, "Lo, I want to make love." Because I was in caretaker mode, making love was the last thing on my mind.

I said, "Naw, bae, let's wait until you feel better."

"Lo, I want to make love as long as I have strength," he said.

"Okay," I said reluctantly because it was what he wanted and needed. Taking care of him was not just about his physical health, but it was about his spiritual and mental health as well. He assured me that he was fine and that was what he wanted to do. "Okay, but I'm on top," I said. Until then, not being able to be on top was not an issue for him but it had come to that stage in our love making. At the start of us making love, I was conflicted in how I should feel because I did not think it was appropriate for me to enjoy my husband in that way, knowing that he could be dying; but once we got into it, I let myself go and enjoyed every minute of it because I know that's what he wanted me to do. "Vincent, how do you feel when you come?" I asked while we were lying in bed after making love because I know the heart rate goes up and the breathing gets rapid when having an orgasm. I wanted to know how he did it.

"When I come, I have to hold back. I can't just let myself go like usual," he said. Because of the strength he had, it was not reasonable to me at the time to do as the hospice nurse suggested: that he should not seek treatment but that he should die. I know those were not her exact words but again, that's what I heard.

When his friend Victor returned with Vincent Jr., he came in with a bouquet of flowers and said, "Brother, I speak life. You are going to live and not die. These flowers are in celebration of your life." He went on exalting the name of the Lord and speaking positive words of encouragement. After all the talk and conversations about dying, it was refreshing to have the energy and spirit of life that he ushered into our apartment.

Chapter 20

Celebration of Life

Saturday night, April 19, 2014, Vincent was in excruciating pain and could not sleep. I remember that date because the next day was our oldest granddaughter's birthday, and Easter Sunday. He was up and down all night, trying to sleep, but the pain was unbearable. "Where does it hurt at?" I asked.

"Right here on my side," he said while standing in the bathroom doorway with his hand on the area the pain was emanating from. I was sleepy but I did not want to fall asleep while he was in so much pain and I remember looking at him with blurred vision wondering what I could do to help him.

"Bae come lay down," I said. I put on some worship music and he leaned back in the bed, but he did not fully lay down. I reached over and placed my hand on the area of his side where he said the pain was. We both dozed off for about an hour while the music played, but soon after the music stopped, Vincent was up again. This went on until about 5am that morning. "Bae, you want to go to the hospital?" I asked.

"Yeah, the pain won't go away," he said. We went to the hospital and Vincent was diagnosed with pneumonia again and he was admitted to the hospital. They quickly got the pain under control and after they put him in a room, I left the hospital to cook Easter dinner for him and my family. After I finished cooking, I fixed Vincent a plate and went back to the hospital. The kids and grandkids came up later so that we could celebrate our granddaughter's birthday together.

Again, after a couple of days of being in the hospital, Vincent began to feel much better. He also had visits from his coworkers. The love and concern that his coworkers showed overwhelmed me, and I started crying. While shedding a few tears himself, Vincent said, "You all just don't know what your visits mean to me." I saw what he meant when he called his coworkers his Invacare family because they came in groups: four or more at a time, even those who worked in the front office. Also, a couple of them who had retired came to visit him as well. Their visits showed me that the feelings he had towards them were mutual; they were his Invacare family.

Vincent stayed in the hospital for about five days before he was discharged to go home. "You're ready to fight with me one more day?" I asked him each morning as I gave him a kiss.

"Yeah," he responded. I knew it was getting tough for him to keep fighting because whenever he went to the hospital and received medicine for pneumonia, he started feeling better only to return home and have the symptoms return. It was as if someone hit the replay button. The pain returned slightly, and he started retaining fluid around his waist which was something different. The cancer doctor who saw Vincent in the hospital asked him to make an appointment at her office and he did. Vincent, Victor (his brother), and I went to the doctor's appointment. The doctor wanted Vincent to try a new medicine that she thought might help him. "I don't want to keep putting my family through this, getting their hopes up only to be let down; I don't want to try the new medicine," he said. The doctor was disappointed in his decision not to go for more treatment, but she accepted it.

"Vincent, you don't want to try the medicine?" I asked.

"Lo, I can't keep putting y'all through that," he said.

I selfishly wanted to say, 'We're fine, we'll go through it if it means keeping you here with us,' but my response was simply, "Okay."

Besides, I knew he was tired of the rollercoaster ride of feeling better, then feeling sick, again and again.

After returning home from the doctor's appointment, I left Vincent and Victor in our bedroom talking while I took the trash down to the dumpster at the apartment complex. While walking, I heard the thought, "Have a celebration of life," and I thought about when his friend Victor brought the flowers and said, 'These flowers are in celebration of your life.' When I returned from taking out the trash, I went where Vincent and Victor were in the bedroom and excitedly said, "We should have a celebration of life for you, Vincent!"

"Sis, that's a good idea but we have to do it soon before I leave," Victor said because he was scheduled to go back to Turkey in a couple of days.

"The thought came to me while I was taking out the trash," I excitedly said. Vincent did not say anything, but tears started rolling down his face. That was not the reaction I expected from him because I was still not facing the reality that he could die, I just wanted to celebrate his life. But when he started crying, I saw the thought did not invoke excitement for him but instead, sadness. If I had known he was going to cry, I would not have said it. "Bae, this does not mean I believe you're dying; we're going to celebrate your life while you're here and that's a good thing," I said. At the time, I really did not think Vincent was going to die. Still not saying anything, he continued to wipe the tears from his eyes.

I left Vincent and Victor at the house again to pick up his prescriptions from the store and as I was driving, the Lord began to speak to me. He told me who would speak at Vincent's funeral and I started crying because God was plainly letting me know that Vincent was going to die. When I started crying, the Holy Spirit took over and I began to speak in tongues, and it continued until I arrived at the store. Before getting out of the car, I cleaned my face because I didn't want anyone to know I had been crying. As I walked in the store to pick up Vincent's prescription, everything went dark and I felt my body go limp. Why did I not end up on the floor passed out, I do not know; but when I came to myself, I saw one of the mothers from my church. She walked up to me and we started talking. I did not inform her of what had just happened to me but keeping my composure while I spoke with her was difficult because I could not wait to get back to my car to cry.

"How is Deacon Paige?" she asked me.

I wanted to say, 'Mother, he's dying,' but I said, "He's alright. I am here picking up his medicine." Her husband had cancer as well so we encouraged each other, and I left the store. When I got back in my car, the weeping started; and again, the Holy Spirit did too. He continued until I arrived home. That is when I noticed that each time I cried when I was alone, the Holy Spirit took over and I began to speak in tongues.

I did not say anything to anyone about what God had said to me about Vincent's funeral or that I felt faint when I went to pick up his medicine. Saturday came and I noticed Vincent laying around more than usual. Not knowing who to call but needing someone to talk to, I grabbed the phone and went into the closet in our bedroom to be discreet because I didn't want Vincent to hear me. The only person I thought of calling was one of my close friends who went to our church. After we said our hellos, I bluntly said, "My husband is dying." I know that it was a little heavy to lay on her, but I did not know who else to call and I did not know how else to say it. After slight hesitation, she began to speak words of encouragement to me, and she let me know she was there for me.

A little later that day, Vincent, Victor, and our two sons walked to the pool area at our apartment complex and sat and talked for a while. Vincent's sisters, Lisa and Stacy, came over a little later and we walked to the pool area where they were. As we walked up,

Victor said, "Sis, Vince didn't even know who you were. He wanted to know who that was with Lisa and Stacy."

"Oh, you don't know your own wife?" I asked laughing.

"Yeah, I just couldn't tell that was you," he said. I was in the process of doing my hair and I had hair extensions in it, so maybe that's why he did not know who I was. We laughed it off and I returned home to finish doing my hair while they were at the pool. Even when he was not feeling the best, he always put the best on the outside. I know he did not feel good, but he wanted to hang out with his family around the pool and they were there for about two hours.

When Vincent returned to the apartment, he started laying around again and I lay with him. While we were in bed, my pastor's wife called and she asked me, "How are you doing?"

"I'm fine," I said.

"Do you need anything?" she asked.

"I just want my husband to get better," I answered.

"Awww, I know, Lo. I'm praying for you all," she said.

Later that evening, Vincent started having the excruciating pain again. The next morning, which was a Sunday, Vincent called his primary doctor about the pain and he said to meet him at his office. He came in on a Sunday and wrote Vincent a prescription for the pain. I had never seen a doctor go to such lengths for his patients. He had even made a house call to our apartment to bring Vincent a respirator until hospice brought one out to help Vincent with shortness of breath. I know house calls may have been common practice back in the day, but it was not common practice at that time. I am sure he knew Vincent was dying, but he still went the extra mile to take care of his patient. It was difficult for us to find a pharmacy to fill the prescription, but after going to two or three, we finally found one that could fill it and we got the medicine. The pain medicine was in the form of a patch that had to be worn for a week and at the end of the week, it had to be changed. Thankfully, the pain patch did the trick and Vincent did not have any more pain; but he slept more than usual for the first couple of days of wearing the patch, which concerned me. But after a couple of days, he was back to his normal sleep pattern. It must have taken his body time to get acclimated to the medicine.

A few days later, Vincent and I were laying on our backs in bed with our legs hanging off the edge of the bed, talking and holding hands when suddenly Vincent sat up and he had a staunch gaze in his eyes. "Vincent, what's wrong?" I asked, but he was unable to respond and continued with the gaze. Then I noticed that he could not breathe. It was as if his breath was cut off, like he was choking on something. "Victor, Poogy, come here!" I yelled. Victor and Vincent Jr. came into the room and Victor started hitting Vincent in the back to get him to breathe. "Breathe, bae, breathe," I said as Victor continued hitting him in the back.

"Come on Vince, breathe," Victor said. After what seemed like five minutes (but it was probably more like a minute), Vincent coughed up clots of blood and started taking breaths. In the meantime, I had called 911 and they were on their way. When they got to the apartment, they came in and did what they do, and said Vincent needed to go to the hospital. Vincent walked out to the ambulance, and they put him in the back and proceeded to the hospital. Victor and I followed along in the car.

Vincent was admitted to the hospital again and they began treating him for pneumonia; and again, he began to feel better. The analogy that the hospice nurse used about plugging up one leak and then another one appears started becoming reality for me. However, I was willing to continue plugging the leaks if it allowed me more time with my husband. His primary doctor came to see him along with the cancer doctor.

A pulmonologist also came in to see him. He took more chest x-rays and walking into the room holding the results, he said, "I don't know how you are still alive. These are your lungs and this is the cancer," he said while holding the pictures of Vincent's lungs so that we could view them. He went on to say, "The tumor seems to be growing out of itself." I did not know what he meant by that statement but from looking at the pictures, it was plain to see that the cancer almost covered Vincent's lungs. A couple of days later, the pulmonologist came back to see Vincent and he wanted to take more pictures to see if he could determine where the blood was coming from that was coming up whenever Vincent coughed. After the pictures were taken, he came into the room and showed us those pictures as well, and the fresh red blood was flowing but he did not know the origin of it. To see where the blood was coming from required Vincent to have surgery and the pulmonologist suggested that he go to Shands Hospital in Gainesville to have it done.

"No, I'm not going to Gainesville away from my family," Vincent said shooting that suggestion down quickly. "If I'm going to die, I want to be near my family."

Invacare had told Vincent to let them know if there was anything they could do for him. Vincent had mentioned to them that he might need a hospital bed if his condition worsened because Invacare made them. One morning before I was preparing to leave home to go up to the hospital, Vincent called and said, "Lo, some of the guys from the job are coming to the apartment to bring a hospital bed this morning." The guys came with the bed, which was still in the box and needed to be assembled. They took the parts out of the box and assembled the bed so it would be ready for Vincent when he came home from the hospital. I know I said it previously, but I must say it again: my heart was overwhelmed with the love and support shown to our family by Invacare during that time.

The hospital staff moved Vincent to a larger room because of the number of visitors he had. Victor was still staying with Vincent at night, and I stayed with him during the day. One night as I was preparing to leave, Vincent said, "Lo, I want you to stay with me tonight."

Victor looked at Vincent and said, "Well, I guess we'll both be here tonight cause I'm staying too."

"You want me to stay?" I asked.

"Yeah, I feel a little funny," he responded.

"Okay, I'll stay," I said.

Then after a few minutes, Vincent said, "Lo, you can go, I think I'll be alright."

"You sure?" I asked.

"Yeah, I'll be alright," he said. I did not know what he meant when he said he felt funny so with some reluctance, I went home and Victor stayed with him. When I arrived at his room the next morning, I asked, "Why did you want me to stay?"

"Lo, I was feeling funny and I did not know if I would make it through the night. I want you to be with me if that happens," he said. He thought he was going to die that night and that's why he wanted me to stay with him. Thank God he made it through that night and greeted me with a smile and a kiss the next morning.

The following Thursday, Victor was scheduled to leave on a flight back to Turkey. He had planned to leave earlier, but he had to reschedule the flight because Vincent went to the hospital. On the Saturday before Victor's flight was scheduled to leave he said, "Hey, Sis, we have to have the celebration of life before I leave." Honestly, I was procrastinating having the celebration of life because deep down, I knew my husband was dying and I knew that was why God told me to have the celebration of life for him. It wasn't an exciting thought anymore and I did not want to do it. That is why I know this was all orchestrated by God. God knew how I felt about all of this, and he had Victor there to make sure I did what He wanted me to do.

"Okay, let's do it tomorrow. I'll send out texts to everyone to let them know and we'll do it here in the hospital," I said.

With short notice, those who we notified about the celebration of life came to the hospital. That included Vincent's mom and all his siblings who were in town, except Eric; he had come to visit Vincent at the hospital the previous day. Also, his nephews and my sisters Gail and Jonita came. I had called Fantasy early that morning and told her to bring a cake and flowers, and his sister Denise brought flowers as well. Altogether, there were about twenty of us in Vincent's hospital room. I did not know how this celebration of life was going to happen, but it had to happen. The hospital staff, believing Vincent needed a bigger room because of all his visitors, put him in the perfect room to have the celebration.

"Thank you all for coming," I began as I explained that our purpose for being there was to celebrate Vincent's life and to let him know how much we love him and how much he means to us. Being the first to speak, I started by saying, "Vincent you are the love of my life and you have made my life so sweet." Through my tears, I went on to say other things which I cannot recall but I know I said, "Thank you for being the best husband, friend, and lover I could ever want." Then my mother-in-law said a few words and it continued around the room as each person said something if he or she wanted to.

"I'm not gonna say anything right now because I know I'll get too emotional," Victor said, but he did not have to say anything because he showed Vincent how much he loved him and how much he meant to him. I am sure that while in private, he shared his feelings with him. Delrick, Fantasy, and Vincent Jr. all told their dad what he meant to them and how much they loved him. Denise spoke words of encouragement because she had a bout with cancer also. Inez, Lisa, Stacy, and Stanley along with the nephews and then my sisters Gail and Jonita all told Vincent how much he meant to them.

Lastly, it was Vincent's turn to speak. Wiping the tears from his eyes, he started by saying, "Lo, you are my hero. You have been by my side and hung in there with me through it all." He said some other words to me and then he spoke to his mom, our children, his siblings, my siblings and his nephews, letting them know how much they meant to him and that he loved them all. Then we held hands and sang, "I Speak Life" by Donald Lawrence. Afterwards, we had cake while we laughed and talked with each other. It was a beautiful time.

"Loretta this was nice, we should've recorded this," Lisa said. She was right because memory in no way does justice to the celebration of life we had for him. I had never seen or been a part of any such celebration ever.

Chapter 21

"That Time" Came

Vincent was discharged from the hospital the following Wednesday and he was feeling somewhat better. We arrived home and he sat in his recliner in the living room. Two of his coworkers, Irma and Cynthia, stopped by and visited with him for a few minutes. Vincent called those two coworkers along with another coworker named Olga his "Angels" like the television show Charlie's Angels. He said when he saw them each morning, they would say, "Good morning, Charlie," and he would respond, "Hello, Angels." They had a great working relationship and friendship. Cynthia was known for baking cakes for the Christmas holidays, and I would get so excited to see him walk in with some of her delicious red velvet cupcakes.

"Look what I got," he would say as he walked in the house with cupcakes in hand.

And I would excitedly say, "Yay!"

While they were visiting, Vincent said, "Lo, go get them pictures of my lungs." He wanted them to see the results of the x-rays that showed the widespread growth of the cancer in his lungs and what the doctors said about not knowing how he is still alive. I could tell that they did not know how to respond to seeing the pictures or his comments, but he wanted his extended Invacare family to know what was happening to him.

Delrick came over later with Tamika and our granddaughters and the oldest one wasn't doing what she was supposed to be doing in school. After hearing what happened, Vincent sternly said, "Lauryn, you better go to school, listen to your teacher and do your schoolwork, you hear me?"

"Yes," she responded. He was not feeling the best but he was still granddad, and Lauryn knew granddad meant what he said.

Victor and Vincent Jr. had gone to the store to get some meat to put on the grill. "Bae, you wanna go for a walk?" I asked Vincent.

"Yeah, we can go for a walk," he responded. We went for a short walk to the pond near our apartment and back. With the breathing tubes in his nostrils and rolling the oxygen tank along as we walked, Vincent said, "Lo, I look in the mirror and I see what's going on with my body. I can see that I'm losing weight."

"I see it too, bae, but I can't go by what it looks like," I said because it was still difficult for me to accept that he was dying.

"I know but whatever God' will is for me, I'm alright with it," he said. He made it clear to me that if it was God's will for him to die, he was at peace with it.

When Victor and Vincent Jr. finished cooking, we ate dinner and Vincent must have had an appetite because he ate more that evening than he had eaten in a couple of weeks. We sat around and talked for a while. Delrick and his family left to go home, and Vincent and I prepared to get ready for bed while Victor and Vincent Jr. were still watching the television. Standing in the mirror, looking at himself Vincent said, "Lo, I need a haircut, but I don't feel like it tonight. I'll let you cut it tomorrow."

"Okay," I said. I am not a barber but Vincent taught me how to use his clippers to cut all his hair off, which is how he had been cutting his hair for a few years. He said since he cut it all off, there was no need to go the barber for that. He only went to the barber to shape his mustache and chin hair.

Then he proceeded to sit on the toilet to urinate because he said standing to urinate exhausted him. After going to the bathroom, he came and sat on the bed and he calmly said, "Lo, I don't know what happened when I peed, but something does not feel right."

"How do you feel?" I asked as I sat down next to him. Vincent might have known what was happening but to keep me calm, he did not bluntly say it.

"I don't know, but something happened when I peed," he said. Then he started coughing up quite a bit of blood, so much so that I got a cup for him to spit in because he could not keep walking to the bathroom. Sitting on the edge of the bed, he laid his head on my shoulder while we held each other's hand and rubbed our feet together. The atmosphere was tranquil as we sat there not saying much, just holding each other. After sitting there for an hour or so, Vincent said, "Something is going on, I don't know what it is, but you might need to call hospice."

"Wait, bae, don't panic," I said.

"I'm not panicking, Lo, but something is happening." He was not the one panicking, I was. I believed if hospice got involved, then that meant death was soon, and I was not ready to concede to death. So as far as I was concerned, hospice was the enemy. Nevertheless, Vincent was adamant about calling hospice because he knew that there was something going on in his body that he had not felt before, and it was not good.

I called hospice and we sat and waited for the nurse to arrive. Victor walked back and forth between our bedroom and the other bedroom checking on Vincent. Vincent Jr. was also in the other bedroom with Victor. By the time the hospice nurse arrived, Vincent's breathing was noticeably hampered. The nurse suggested to Vincent to take some medicine she had that was in pill form, but Vincent could not swallow the pill. "I can't take that pill because I can't breathe. I wanna go to the hospital," he said.

The hospice nurse insisted that if he took the pill, it would help him. "Didn't you hear me? I can't breathe, I can't swallow the pill," Vincent said insistently.

"If he can't take the pill, then he needs to go the hospital," the hospice nurse said reluctantly, so we called 911. Vincent's ability to breathe was lessening by the second and it seemed as if the EMT's were not coming fast enough.

Victor was in the bedroom with us and he said, "Let's take him ourselves." While we were loading Vincent in the car, the emergency vehicle pulled up and they took Vincent to the hospital.

I followed the ambulance in my car and Victor and Vincent Jr. followed in another car. After checking in at the emergency room, the hospital staff allowed us to go back and see Vincent. When I walked in the room and looked in my husband's eyes, which were barely open, I saw death and I knew this was it; my husband was leaving me. With the bed propped up to an almost sitting position, he was lying there with his head hanging down, chin towards his chest because he was too weak to hold his head up. I do not know what happened in the ambulance from our apartment to the hospital, which was only about five minutes away. When the EMT put Vincent in the ambulance, he was fully awake and responsive. In fact, he was still able to walk.

When I walked into the hospital room, he hardly acknowledged that I was there. "Hey, bae," I said as I approached the bed. He nodded his head in acknowledgement, but he could not say anything. The EMT must've had him hooked up to oxygen while being transported to the hospital because he still had a mouthpiece between his lips, but nothing was connected to it, so I removed the piece from his mouth. Vincent was extra calm and peaceful, no longer complaining about not being able to breathe. It was as if he was sitting, patiently waiting for what was going to happen.

"Da," Vincent Jr. said as he walked in the room calling out to his dad. I walked out of the room leaving Vincent Jr. with his dad and started making phone calls to family. First, I called Delrick, and Fantasy and told them their dad was in the emergency room and they needed to come to the hospital because it did not look good. Then I started calling other family members. "We're at the hospital with Vincent and I think this is it," I said to my sister Gail.

"Okay, I'm coming," she said. Victor was also making phone calls to the family.

Calling Jonita, I said, "Hey, we're at the hospital with Vincent and it doesn't look good."

Since she lived close to my mother-in-law, she said, "I'll catch a ride up there with Stacy and Ms. Annie Ruth." Although it was already after midnight, I decided to call our pastor to let him know just in case he wanted to come to see Vincent because from what I saw in my husband's eyes, I thought that would be the last time we would see him alive.

I walked back into Vincent's room and Vincent Jr. was still in there with him, wiping his face with a wet cloth. The hospice nurse was also still there with us. Family members started coming in to see Vincent and for some it was difficult to see him like that. Victor was in and out of the room, and it seemed like he just could not stop moving.

Later, the hospital staff reclined Vincent to a fully lying position with a pillow under his head and connected him to oxygen because his body was only producing a minimal amount. The concentrator machine was loud and the mask covering his nose and his mouth connecting him to the machine seemed tight and uncomfortable. Then I later saw that the attendant had not positioned the oxygen mask correctly because it only covered his top lip and it should have covered his entire mouth, so I repositioned it. With the loud oxygen machine going along with the uneasiness I was feeling, the ambience was not as peaceful as it was before.

Delrick and Fantasy arrived at the hospital. After checking on their dad, Delrick stayed in the room with Vincent Jr. and Fantasy followed me because it was hard for me to sit still. Also, our pastor had arrived at the hospital. The doctor came into the room and said he needed to get a chest tube into Vincent because his lung had collapsed. Then one of the nurses said to me, "He's dying; let him die with dignity." She did not think we should do anything for Vincent because he was going to die no matter what. At that point, I was confused because if the doctor thinks a chest tube will help Vincent, then do it. On the other hand, I was not sure if Vincent wanted that. It is my belief that he knew it was time and he was ready, but I was not ready.

Along with our daughter and our pastor, I walked to Vincent's bed sobbing, and I said, "Vincent, tell me what to do; tell me what to do." But he could not respond to me.

"They say when hospice comes in, all they do is give you medicine, so you no longer have the fight to live," I said to Vincent one day while we were having a conversation about hospice.

"Well, Lo when that time comes, I want the meds and I wanna be home," he emphatically said.

"Okay," I said and I believed 'that time' was the present time. Still, I was grasping for hope and if anyone offered any kind of hope, I seized it. I told the doctor to go ahead with the chest tube and he did; but because the cancer was so dense in Vincent's chest, he could not insert the chest tube. I thought to myself, "It wasn't supposed to be" and I kept hearing in my head, the nurse saying, 'Let him die with dignity.'

"Do you want us to resuscitate him if he stops breathing?" the doctor asked.

Shaking my head, I said, "No, he doesn't want to be resuscitated."

When Vincent's primary doctor walked into the emergency room, he looked at Vincent's vitals and he said, "You know what's happening now don't you? He's dying." Victor was sitting in the room with Vincent but when the doctor said that, he suddenly jumped up and ran out of the room, crying and hyperventilating. Several people went behind Victor to make sure he was all right and he was, once he settled down. I believe hearing the doctor say those words made it all real; Vincent was really leaving us.

Vincent was admitted to the hospital and they put him in a regular room, which was fitting for us as we all wanted to be with him. Later, we noticed that the room was unusually warm, especially for a hospital. The cause of the warmth could have been because there were so many of us gathered in one room, but we informed the hospital staff that we believed the room was too warm and expected them to do something about it, but they did nothing. The minutes turned into hours as we kept watch with him waiting for something to happen. It was uneasy for me to sit so periodically, I walked out of the room to do something, if only to walk down the corridor.

On one of those walks out of the room, I went to the bathroom. While I was there, I was talking to God and I said, "God, if you're gon' take him, go ahead and take him."

"Ma," I heard while coming out of the bathroom. "Da woke up and he wants you," Delrick said meeting me in the corridor.

"He woke up?" I asked.

"Yeah, and he wants you," Delrick said.

"What happened?" I asked as we hurried to the room.

"He woke up, took the oxygen off and asked for you," Delrick said. When I walked in the room, he did not have oxygen on, and he was laying in the bed with one leg up on the bed bent at the knee. I grabbed him by that knee and I began sobbing because I thought that maybe God was giving him back to us.

Vincent sat up in bed and everyone at one time began asking him how he was feeling. "I feel alright," he said. He began scooting to the edge of the bed as if he was trying to get up. "No Vincent, you can't get up," some began to say.

"Relax, relax, I'm not bout to get up," he said. He sat at the edge of the bed and while he was sitting up, he asked for something to drink.

At the same time, his primary doctor walked into the room. "Doctor, he's sitting up and he wants something to drink," we said.

The doctor handed him an Ensure and said, "See if he will drink this," and he did.

Thinking that Vincent was doing better, some family members left and went home. For about an hour, we had Vincent back with us. Then he began feeling weak again and we helped him rest back in bed as he was before. After the shift change, one of the nurses who knew Vincent well came to see him when she heard he was there and that he was dying. She informed me that one of the other nurses went home when she heard what was happening with Vincent because it was too overwhelming for her.

The nurse who came to see him visited for a few minutes and when she left, I walked with her out of the room and said, "Listen, I know they think my husband is dying and him being in a cooler room is not a priority. But I wish they could find a cooler room for him; the room is too warm." She did not comment on what I said about the warmth of the room, but it was not much longer that I was told they were moving Vincent to another room, and it was so much cooler and even bigger than the one he was in before.

While they were getting Vincent set up in the cooler room, someone from administration spoke to me about setting up with hospice either to take Vincent to their facility or to come home with him when he was discharged from the hospital. I was still rejecting hospice because I was still rejecting the thought of my husband dying, so I did not immediately give consent for hospice. "He's not going to a facility. If they come, Vincent will be home," I said. I did not want hospice for my husband, so the person I spoke with told me to think about it and let her know my decision. When I went back to the room, I told the family that they wanted to contact hospice so they could come to the house for Vincent, and I must give them my decision.

"Come on, Lo, I'll go with you," my sister Tammy said. We walked to the office and there were two women in there, the one who I initially spoke with and another one. They were both genuinely pleasant and patient with me as they explained that it was the best thing to do.

"I just don't like hospice, it's like the death angel coming to take my husband," I said.

"Listen to what you just said. It is like an angel that will wait with your husband until his time," one of the women said. Eventually, I consented, and the two women were pleased. They began preparing with transportation to take Vincent home and have hospice to be there when he arrived.

Chapter 22

Waiting for the End

I walked behind the bed as the transportation drivers rolled Vincent down the hospital halls. Several people walked past us, and I was hoping someone would hear me silently screaming for help to save my husband's life.

The pulmonologist who had seen Vincent in the hospital saw us and he asked, "Is that Mr. Paige?"

"Yes," I responded, hoping he was the one to help us.

"How is he doing?" he asked.

"He's going home with hospice. Is there anything you can do for him?" I asked.

He shook his head and said, "No."

"Okay," I said, and we continued down the halls and out of the hospital.

Vincent Jr. met his dad outside our apartment and walked beside the bed as the drivers pushed the bed down the sidewalk to the apartment. The bed was propped up, so Vincent was sitting up. As he walked beside the bed, Vincent Jr. asked, "Da, you see the tennis courts?"

"Uh huh," he responded. Those were the tennis courts where he and his dad had played tennis often. Vincent Jr. asked the question because he wanted to see if his dad was alert to his surroundings and he was.

Fantasy was also at the apartment to wait for the hospice nurse just in case she arrived before we did. Hospice had previously delivered an oxygen concentrator to the apartment before Vincent's last visit to the hospital. Vincent was pleased to see that the concentrator was from the company where he was employed. "Poogy, that's an Invacare concentrator there; that's one of ours," he proudly said.

The hospice nurse met us at the apartment and hospice delivered a second oxygen concentrator because it was determined that one was not sufficient for Vincent's respiratory needs. The transportation drivers transferred Vincent to his bed and after getting him settled in, they turned on the oxygen concentrators and placed the nose canula in his nostrils. The concentrators were in our bedroom but because of the heat generated by the machines, we decided to put the machines in the bathroom and close the bathroom door so that the bedroom would not get too warm for Vincent's comfort.

We got Vincent settled in and the waiting began. I was hoping we were waiting for God to perform a miracle and heal Vincent of the cancer instead of waiting for him to die. "Baby, you're home like you said you wanted to be," I said to Vincent and he nodded his head in agreement. It was well into the evening, and family and friends came in and out checking on Vincent and us. Vincent was not alert much at all; in fact, he slept a lot. The hospice nurse was there and she wanted to give him some meds, but I did not give consent for her to give Vincent any meds since he was already sleeping. As the night went on, Vincent woke up and tried to get out of bed. "Vincent, where are you going?" I asked.

"I got to pee," he said while sitting up in bed.

"Well, you can't get out of bed," I said.

He asked, "Why?"

Not knowing how to answer him, I said, "Okay, we'll help you," and the nurse said it was okay. We were all in the room, Victor, Vincent Jr., Fantasy, and me. Victor and I stood him up to help him to the restroom but when we stood him up, he was too weak to stand and sat back on the bed. After that happened, the nurse suggested that he wear adult diapers, so we put him on a diaper. Out of instinct, Vincent tried to get up at least two more times during the night to go pee. "Vincent, you don't have to go the bathroom, you can stay here in bed and pee," I said.

None of us slept that night because Vincent was up and down all night. Fantasy and I slept in our bed with me, and Vincent Jr. slept on the floor beside his dad's hospital bed. Each time we heard Vincent move, we were up. "Da, Da," Vincent Jr. called to his dad each time he heard him wake up as if he was waiting on him to move so that he could say something to him.

On one of those instances, Vincent sat up in bed for a few minutes. We tried to get him to lay down, but he was not having it; he would not lay back in bed. He sat up and held on to the bed rail because he was not ready to lay back down. Then when he was ready, he lay back in the bed. On another occasion he sat up, grabbed Vincent Jr. by the hand and said, "My boy, my boy." I did not know what Vincent's mental state was at that moment and although I had not consented for the hospice nurse to administer any meds yet, she asked if she could give him something to help him sleep, and I consented. Vincent and the others slept, but I still could not sleep, so I went into the living room and kept company with the hospice nurse.

The morning came and we were still waiting. Vincent did not wake up much that day and it looked like death was imminent. I went to take a shower and said, "Lord, if you gon' take him, go ahead and take him because it's hard seeing him like this." To watch the love of my life at only forty-eight years old, a man who was so full life, now lying at the brink of death was physically and emotionally draining. I did not know what or how to feel or what to do. After my shower, I lay down and dozed off to sleep for a few minutes as family and friends came in and out, off and on throughout the day. I did get some alone time with Vincent and kneeling beside his bed, I grabbed his hand and began to pray.

With my heart slowly crumbling, I began to say, "Lord, if it's possible, let this cup pass from me; but nevertheless, not my will, but thy will be done." I continued crying and praying as the Holy Spirit took over and interceded for me. It was a garden of Gethsemane moment for me because I was saying to God that His will was so much greater than my will, and I accept His will even if it meant Vincent was going to die. While I was praying, Vincent looked at me with clear eyes that were full of life and strength. I saw my husband and I had not seen him for almost twenty-four hours, although I was with him the entire time. "Vincent, I love you, I love you!" I cried out to him. I wanted to hear him say, 'Lo, I love you too.' And I know if he could have, he would have. He continued to watch me as I cried and prayed. It reminded me of the first time our eyes met when he was trying to get my attention with that sexy smile that said *hello* while sitting in the back seat of Nita's car as me and her stopped briefly to speak to each other in the parking lot at my mom's apartment. Only this time, he was saying *goodbye* because that was the last time he opened his eyes. After praying, I lay back in the bed and dozed off again.

As the evening went on, family and loved ones came to check on Vincent. Then the night came, and everyone was gone. Of course the hospice nurse was still there along with me, Fantasy, Vincent Jr., Victor, and Delrick. About three o'clock in the morning, a new hospice nurse came. She went in and checked on Vincent and noticed his breathing was labored, so she wanted to give him some more medicine. "May I give him some medicine to calm him down?" she asked.

I had heard Vincent's breathing but because I was still wary about the medicine, I procrastinated in giving her an answer. "Ma, you know he said to give him the medicine," Fantasy said. Reluctantly, I did what he wanted me to do and consented for the nurse to administer the medicine. But when she gave it to him, his breathing did not calm down at all; in fact, it got worse. Vincent started taking deep, long breaths and the time in between each breath started getting longer.

"It's time; he's leaving," the hospice nurse said standing at his bed side. I called Victor, Delrick and Vincent Jr. into the room and we all stood around his bed. As Vincent took one final breath, the nurse took his blood pressure, checked his pulse, and said, "He's gone."

I had my hand on his heart and I still felt it beating so in response, I said, "Not yet, I still feel his heart beating."

"Okay," the nurse said.

I kept my hand on his heart until the last heartbeat and then I said, "Okay, he's gone," and the nurse called his death at 3:30am.

"It wasn't because of the medicine," the nurse said to me because she knew what I thought about the medicine.

"Oh, I know it wasn't the medicine," I said to her assuredly. "D, call Tamika and the girls," I said to Delrick.

"You want them to come?" he asked.

"Yes, I want them here," I said. Victor called the family and I called my family as well to let them know Vincent was gone. I remember telling Vincent that I could not watch him die but by the grace of God, I did. I would not have wanted it any other way because I saw that death was not something to fear. Vincent not only showed me how to live but he also showed me how to die.

In his acceptance of God's will for him, I saw him live unto God and I saw him die unto God. For me to be there when that beautiful soul took his last breath and to feel the last beat of his heart is an experience I will always treasure. The peace of God, the Comforter, blanketed me and held me mightily. I am forever grateful to God for allowing me to be there with him, holding his hand and touching his heart as his life here on earth ended.

Tamika and our granddaughters along with Vernice, Tamika's mother, were the first ones to arrive at the apartment. Vernice stayed the night with Tamika and the girls for support because Delrick stayed with us at the apartment to be with his dad. "Bye, Granddad," each of our granddaughters said as they touched his hand. Tamika held his hand and said bye as well.

"Can I touch him?" Vernice asked.

"Sure," I said. She grabbed Vincent's hand and began thanking him for being such a wonderful grandfather to her grandbabies and a wonderful father-in-law to her daughter. "I have never touched a dead person because I was always scared, but this is so peaceful," she said.

Vincent's mother and siblings all came over when they got the call. My mother-in-law walked into the bedroom crying. I can only imagine the grief she felt, knowing she would never be able to talk to her son or feel the love from his hugs and kisses again. Some of my sisters came over as well and for a moment, we all gathered around Vincent's bed, held hands and thanked God for Vincent's life and prayed for His continual comfort to keep us.

The hospice nurse who was with Vincent the last time he went to the hospital came and relieved the nurse who was there when Vincent died. She came in and began disposing of all his pain medications. Then she said, "I have to get him ready to go to the funeral home."

"I wanna help you," I said.

"Okay," she responded. I did not know if it was customary or not for the wife or family members to assist in that process; but that was my husband and if he was leaving the house, I wanted to make sure he was dressed for it. As I look back, I think of it as my way to help prepare his body for burial. With the door closed behind us, she said, "We have to wipe him down." I began removing his clothes and we continued to wipe his body down from head to toe. While wiping his hands down, I removed his wedding band from his finger and placed it on my thumb because that was the only finger it fit on my hand. Then we dressed him in clean underclothes, shorts, and a t-shirt. "Do you know which funeral home you are calling?" the hospice nurse asked after we finished wiping him down and dressing him.

"Yes," I responded. She also asked if I needed her to call them. "No, I will call when I am ready for them, and I am not ready yet," I said. Seeming to be impatient just as she was when she wanted Vincent to take that pill that he told her he could not swallow because of his hampered breathing, the nurse wanted me to call the funeral home sooner than later. I did not know if she wanted to be there when they arrived but I told her she could leave and I would call, so she left. By this time, most family members had left. There was only me, Victor, and the children still at the house.

About an hour or so after the nurse left, I called the funeral home and they came to take Vincent. Two guys walked in rolling a gurney on which to put Vincent's body. "Victor, they're getting ready to take him," I said to him.

Victor was lying in bed and said, "Oh, I don't want to see it." The two guys proceeded to roll the gurney into our bedroom and closed the door behind them. Then after about 15 minutes, they opened the door of the bedroom and rolled the gurney out with my husband's body on it. As I sat in the living room and watched them roll the gurney out of the apartment, tears swelled in my eyes. I could not believe it was over, but it was. God had taken the love of my life, and he was never coming back again. I sat there for a few minutes, then I walked into our bedroom, put a sheet on the bed that Vincent had died in, crawled into it, and went to sleep. In the past seventy-two hours, I might have slept ten hours, just getting an hour or two here and there before Vincent died. Trying to sleep did not last long, because once the news of Vincent's death spread we began getting phone calls and visitors.

Vincent died Saturday, May 10, 2014, the day before Mother's Day. The children honored me by giving me a necklace with Vincent's birthstone in it. I was just thankful to have them by my side through it all. That Monday, we went to the funeral home to discuss the business of Vincent's burial. Ms. Eunice, the owner, was pleasant and generous to us.

"So, Ms. Eunice, you've been around here for a while, huh?" Victor asked. Victor never meets a stranger and Ms. Eunice seemed to not mind answering his questions, so Victor and I got a history lesson of Sanford as she talked about the days when they went to the riverfront by horse and buggy to purchase goods from the boats that came in and load them onto the buggies to take the goods home. Preparing for Vincent's funeral with Ms. Eunice was peaceful, insightful, and comical.

Family and friends came over each night before the funeral showing love and support by way of their presence, bringing food, encouragement, laughter, memories and their prayers, which were all very much needed. One evening after family and friends had left, my children and I were sitting in the living room talking about Vincent and as I was sitting on the couch, I saw myself on the floor kicking and screaming. I said to my children, "I just saw myself having a kicking and screaming tantrum on the floor."

"Ma, maybe that's what you need to do," Delrick said because I had not had any public outburst of grief from my husband's death, but I had private outbursts of grief in my daily times with God:

"God, did you have to take him now? God, why did you let him get his arm amputated if he was going to die anyway? God, why did you take us and make us the perfect husband and wife for each other, gave us a marriage that others marveled at and then you take him? Why?" I wanted answers but I did not get them. So yes, I was having some private spiritual temper tantrums with God.

Vincent's funeral was set for Saturday, May 17, 2014. The Thursday before his funeral, we went to view his body at the funeral home before the public viewing, which was scheduled for the following evening. Earlier in the week, I had taken his suit, tie, shirt, and underclothes for the funeral staff to dress him in. The suit he wore was the same suit he wore to our son's wedding because it was my favorite suit.

When Vincent went to purchase that suit, he tried it on, and he started sliding back and forth, dancing like James Brown and looking sexy. "Boy, you betta stop that; I'm ready to take you home," I said as we laughed. I did not know what to expect or how I would feel seeing Vincent in a casket. When I walked in the room, the first thing I noticed was he did not have a haircut, and I said, "Oh, no, y'all have to cut his hair; there is no way you can leave his hair like that."

"Ma, you were gonna cut his hair that night, but he wanted you to wait until morning," Fantasy said.

"Yeah, I know." Surprisingly, it was not a sad occasion and other than his hair, Vincent looked good. He had that same peaceful look he had when I last saw him in bed at home.

We arrived for the public viewing the following day and the funeral home's barber had cut Vincent's hair to my satisfaction. Family and friends started pouring into the hall. I stood over Vincent's body lying in the casket, and I thought I would be overwhelmed with sorrow and grief; but again, it was not a sad occasion for me. Seeing his body left me feeling indifferent, neither sad nor happy, because

I knew that Vincent was no longer in that body. I found myself comforting others who were overwhelmed with grief. It was awe-inspiring seeing each person from different races come up to greet me and then go pay their respects to my husband. I knew of the respect and admiration he had for so many, but to see and hear the respect and admiration so many had for him left me thankful to be his wife and thankful that God favored me with Vincent as my husband.

On the day of the funeral, I started my day as usual in my prayer place to spend time in the presence of God. Karen, Vincent's sister from Rochester came to town. She informed me that she and Vincent had talked before he died and that he told her to come. She had made plans to come see Vincent before he died, but he died before her arrival date. Still, she came and stayed at our apartment. Terdaryle Jr., Vincent's nephew also came, and he stayed with us at the apartment as well, which is what we do during those times. We want and need family to come if they are able and if they need somewhere to stay, we make room for them.

Vincent's funeral was the third funeral at our church that day, so it was scheduled later in the day. The morning was not rushed for me; I had time to eat breakfast and try and relax a bit before the funeral, which I found difficult to do (the relaxing part that is). Then it was time for me to get dressed and because I chose the grey suit for Vincent to wear, we all wore something of color to coordinate with the grey. We also decided to have the family line up and leave for the funeral from my mother-in-law's apartment and to return there after the repast because she had more outdoor area at her apartment to accommodate family and friends.

Dressing for Vincent's funeral was surreal. I knew I was going to a funeral, but it did not feel like it was my husband's funeral. We all gathered at my mother-in-law's apartment and the funeral cars lined up to transport us to the church. After we loaded into the car,

I said to the driver, "It feels like I'm going to someone else's funeral."

"Oh, you will feel like that until you see him; that's how I was when my mother passed," she said. We lined up outside the church and began to walk in behind the ministers and I was fine until I saw my husband lying in that casket at the front of the church. A wave of grief came over me and I could not hold back the tears. It was nothing dramatic, I did not fall out or anything, but it happened just like the driver of the funeral car said it would. The day before, I saw my husband lying in the casket, but I did not feel the grief. But that day, as soon as I caught a glimpse of him, I felt it.

Vincent had a homegoing service that was befitting for him and the life he lived. The church was packed with people from all races whom he had an impact on their lives. At my request, the choir sang "He Loves Us" because that was the last song that I saw Vincent singing and raising his hands in worship to God. Along with the eulogy from our pastor, me, Delrick, Fantasy, Vincent Jr., Tamika, Victor, Lisa, and Gail all spoke at the service. Victor, Vincent's friend spoke and Charles a co-worker, spoke as well. Before I spoke, I had a video shown of Vincent and I at one of our married couples' events singing, "Fool in Love" by Ike and Tina Turner. Vincent had a guitar and he wore one of my wigs with the mushroom style that Laurence Fishburne wore in the movie when he portrayed Ike. I dressed the part of Tina as well with a big hair wig while dancing to the music. We enjoyed ourselves and I wanted everyone to see the fun we had together. Those who attended the funeral enjoyed seeing Vincent in that manner because most did not get to see Vincent letting his hair down and having fun. I wanted them to know that that was my man and although he did not put up with foolishness, he did know how to have fun and we had lots of fun times together.

Vincent's brother Tony came to me after the funeral and said, "Lo, I was not coming today, but Mama told me I needed to be here.

You see, my brothers and sisters are all in my bowels and everything and I did not want to see him like that, but I'm glad I came. To see y'all up there as Ike and Tina did me good, girl. Yeah, I'm glad I came," he said smiling.

Chapter 23

I'm Still Full

We knew Vincent was diagnosed with an aggressive malignant cancer, but his death still shook us because Vincent's life seemed to have so much more relevance. He was that dependable pillar of strength family members counted on to always be there giving guidance and support when needed. He was that church member whom the pastor knew he could call for any reason, and Vincent was going to put in one hundred percent effort to get it done.

One of his coworkers told me that Vincent's name was heard over the PA system several times a day at his job. "Vincent Paige, please call such and such, is heard all day," he said because Vincent was that dependable person to get the job done.

It seemed like Vincent had so much more to give because he gave so much. I'd be driving and see someone walking along the street who looked like they didn't know or care about being in this world, and I'd sarcastically say, "Really God?" thinking, "You took Vincent and left him?"

With my husband gone and trying to live the rest of my life without him, I asked God, "Lord what do I do now? You made me Vincent's wife and you took him." I tried being sociable and continued to go around family and friends, but it was awkward for me. I felt naked and uncovered. It would not have been awkward if he was just not with me at the time, because I've done that before; but he was gone and never coming back. Not only was it awkward for me, but it was awkward for others as well. I walked into a restaurant and saw an acquaintance of ours and she said, "Girl, I'm so used to seeing y'all together, not you by yourself."

"I know," I said because I was not used to being by myself. It was God who transformed my mind and made me Vincent's wife because when I married him, I didn't have the mind of a wife. I still had the mind of being an independent woman that I had before we were married. I had no clue what it was to be a wife and I thought I could get married and continue with that mindset. But God knew that with the mindset I had, the marriage He wanted for us would never come to fruition so He got a hold of me quickly. He tore down everything I thought I was and made me Vincent's wife, not just his roommate with benefits. That was not my plan, that was God's plan; and when He finished with me, I had no problem being that and I had delight in it.

God gave me a love for Vincent I never knew existed. It wasn't a fairy tale type love where Vincent was my knight in shining armor. On the contrary, it was simply pure love although there was nothing simple about it. Through Vincent, God gave me superfluous love; it was more than enough. Several people have asked me if I will ever get married again and honestly, I do not think I will because God had that man to love me thoroughly, so I did not miss anything in our marriage. I have heard women say, next time I get married, it will be for finances or some other reason, but I am not looking for a next time. God gave me everything I ever needed in a husband when he gave me Vincent.

My husband loved me spiritually because he encouraged me to seek God. He was a man who worshipped God and he knew that if he pleased God, he would please me. He knew that he was just a man and that he could not be all I needed. My husband loved me sexually by making our lovemaking about what he could give me, which was pure unfeigned love, and not about what he could get out of it. He loved me financially because when we were not financially well-off and God told me to leave my job, he encouraged me to leave my job. He never told me that I had to find another job and never complained about how we were going to make ends meet. He loved me socially because my happiness was a priority to him and he made sure I enjoyed myself whether we were at parties, on road trips, on cruises, or on our Friday date nights that we looked forward to each week. He loved me intellectually because he wanted me to express my opinions, but he also challenged me in my thoughts and was not hesitant to give me a different perception of the way I saw a situation when I needed one.

"Girl, I'm gon love you so good, you gon be able to live off the memories when I'm gone," is what he told me years before he was diagnosed with the cancer; and through God, he did just that. Vincent was and is still the apple of my eye and I have not seen that man anywhere. I have not seen that pureness, that strength, that confidence, that integrity, all which my husband personified. I didn't know that God was filling me up with enough love to last a lifetime, but He did and I am still full.

The weeks following the funeral, I found myself trying to recapture those last moments we had sitting on the side of the bed, his head leaning on my shoulder and my head leaning on his head while we held hands and softly rubbed our feet together waiting for him to feel better, which is what I was hoping for; but instead, we were waiting for him to die. Those last moments seemed so close in my mind that I felt if I pressed my mind into them hard enough, I could have them again; but the closer my mind got to them, the farther away they seemed to be.

I do not know what I was thinking, but somewhere deep inside, I still had not accepted that Vincent was not coming home. I wanted him to call me so I could hear him say, "What's up baby cakes?" like he did each morning on his break, or get that call in the afternoon informing me of what time he would be home and him asking, "What's for din din?" I wanted Vincent to come back to me, because what was I going to do without my lover, my friend, my confidante, my strength? Who was I going to talk to about not only the good that happens during the day, but also the foolishness?

"Guess what such and such did," I would say to him.

I would continue to tell him what happened, and he would respond, "You kiddin." I got a kick out of hearing him saying that, so I would chuckle when he did. If I couldn't have him back, I thought God would at least let me dream about him and our life together, but that has not been the case. I have not dreamed of him often and the few dreams I have had of him were nothing like our life together.

In one dream I had of him, he came back and I said to him, "Vincent, if you wanted to leave, you did not have to fake your death; you could have just left." In the dream, he did not say anything, he just looked at me. I guess it was easier to think that he left me instead of him being dead. I have a picture of Vincent laying in his casket and for a while, each time I looked at it, I said, "Doggonit, you left me!" It would just come out of my mouth because I couldn't believe he had left me by myself.

Trying to find a routine to fill my days without him has not been easy. My time revolved around Vincent and our grandkids. "Lo, the only thing that bothers me about dying is that I won't be here for my grandbabies," he said because our grandkids were a big part of our lives and he enjoyed being Granddad. We were not the grandparents who took the kids to the park to watch them play but we played along with them, running around playing tag and going up and down the slides with them. We were those grandparents who played hide and seek at our apartment complex, running up and down the stairs, hiding with our grandkids. We were those grandparents who walked to the 7-11 with our grandkids to get Slurpee's and other snacks. We were those grandparents who were at every event, their births, birthday parties, sporting events and school events. And all those who knew Vincent knew about his grandbabies, because he enjoyed talking about them.

A couple of weeks after Vincent's death, the grandkids and I were riding in the car and I started to cry thinking about Vincent. "I miss Granddad so much," I said to them.

Our granddaughter, Morgan responded, "But Grandma, he's still here with us."

Wiping my tears away, I said, "You're right, baby, he is still here with us." I am so thankful that they got to know their granddad and to know that they were his heart. And I am also thankful that although Granddad's gone, they still like hanging out with Grandma sometimes.

I wanted to get back to attending church services and after about a month or so, I decided to go to Wednesday bible study because the crowd was smaller and I thought I could handle the smaller crowd first, then try for the Sunday crowd. While driving to the church, my sister-in-law Lisa called to check on me. We were chatting and I was feeling fine. Then as soon as I pulled into the gates of the church, a wave of sorrow came over me and the fountain of tears started flowing. I stayed in the parking lot, hoping the tears would stop but they would not. "Lisa, I'm trying to go to bible study but I can't do it," I said to her as I began crying.

"Yes you can, Loretta; you can do it," she said.

"No, I can't, I'm leaving," I said as I drove out of the parking lot and went back home. I called my daughter later and told her what happened. I said that when I do go back to church, I will need one of them to come with me. A few weeks later, the three of them came with me to a Sunday morning service and surprisingly, I was fine and did not feel any sadness at all. It must have been that initial feeling of knowing I would have to walk in that church alone without my husband whom I had walked into the church with for over eighteen years.

The one thing that has remained constant in my life is my daily prayer place so that I can spend time in the presence of God, which is not a particular place because I can make that place wherever I need it to be. It's usually the first thing I do in the morning. I don't go about the busyness of my day and then try to fit God in somewhere because being in His presence is the most necessary part of my day. I thank God for having that place because it is in that place that God allowed my broken heart to bleed. If I did not have that place, I don't know what would have become of me.

It was suggested to me that I see a grief counselor after my husband's death, but I did not go to any man, or woman for that matter, to try and make sense of my husband's death. Seeing a grief counselor was not an option for me because I believed the generic treatment from a grief counselor was not what I needed. The only option for me was to go to the source of my joy and my sorrow, and that source was God. It was God who had given me the joy I experienced with Vincent and the sorrow I had because of his death, so He was the only grief counselor I needed. I needed those sessions daily, not once or twice a week. A grief counselor could not have endured me daily, but God did and He welcomed me. "God, you gave me this grief, so I am giving it back to you," is what I said to Him. God allowed me to give my broken heart to Him day after day and in turn, He strengthened me.

I was able to face the public and did not appear to be sorrowful. "Loretta, everyone says you are so strong," my pastor said to me.

"But they don't see me when I'm in prayer," I said to him. They didn't see the broken Loretta crying out to God; instead, what they saw was His strength.

I knew there had to be spiritual significance in my grief, in my tears, in my heartache; because each time I went to God, it was as if He was waiting for me. God did not dry the tears up but He allowed the tears to flow because my tears were not only filled with sorrow, but they were also tears filled with worship and adoration for Him and no one else was worthy of that. He knew beforehand the sorrow I would have from my husband's death because He knew what He had given us. God knew in that sorrow, my worship to Him would be even greater. So when the tears came, whether I was in my prayer place, riding in my car, or cleaning my house, it was as if God swooped down to collect those tears because each time the Holy Spirit began to intercede for me. There had to be more that God wanted from me, and I wanted to give it to Him.

"Loretta, why don't you let me and my wife help you," my pastor said, but they did not give my husband and I the marriage we had, God did. I know they wanted to help me, but I knew that the only one who could help me was God.

I had not even shared with my children how I was feeling because I knew that if I talked about my feelings about losing their dad, I would start sobbing and I did not want to break down and cry out in front of them. I wanted to spare them of that, but I knew they needed to hear it from me. On New Year's Day of 2015, I sat the kids down to talk to them about my feelings of missing their dad and the grief I still felt. They were all there: Delrick, Tamika, Fantasy, Vincent Jr., and my grandchildren. "I want to talk to y'all about your dad," I said and before I could get any more words out of my mouth, the tears started to flow like I knew they would. I'm sure they were not expecting that from me because our New Year's talks are usually about our goals and plans for the coming year. The mood quickly changed from happy to somber, but I had to let them know how I was feeling.

"You gon cry?" Delrick asked.

"I just miss him so much and my heart won't stop bleeding," I went on to say. Through the tears, I said, "I love y'all and I'm so thankful for you all, but life is just not the same for me without your dad. Sometimes when I'm driving down the road, I just wanna keep driving, but I don't know where to go." By this time, tears had started flowing from their eyes as well. "I don't wanna come back home because he's not here waiting for me; it don't feel like home because he's not here and my heart hurts so bad," I said to them. After I finished saying what I had to say, Delrick said some words and we all embraced each other and dried our tears. Then the talk went in the direction of goals we had for the new year and our plans for achieving those goals; the talk with them ended happier than it started. I also shared my grief with the women at my church in one of our women's meetings, and I sobbed through that time as well.

Months had passed and my heart was still bleeding. I felt like God owed me something, because I was stuck in a place of profound grief and I couldn't get past it. I wanted something from God, anything that would stop the bleeding. I didn't understand and I wanted answers. I could see if Vincent was a good-for-nothing husband who halfheartedly loved me and his family, then maybe I could have grieved for a while and then moved on but that was not the case. I couldn't move on; my heart was overwhelmed with grief and the tears continued to flow.

"Would it have been better if I had never known Vincent than to have my heart hurt so bad?" I asked God. Then I answered my own question, "But if I had never known him, I would not have experienced Vincent and the love You gave us." When God was transforming us for our marriage, He knew we didn't have time to waste so we had to get it right to enjoy the time we had. God gave us in nineteen years what it takes other couples fifty years or more to achieve in a marriage. Our marriage was the marriage of a lifetime and Vincent was the love of my life.

One day as I was in my prayer place with my husband's death on my mind, this thought came to me: God knew that Vincent was not going to be on this earth long, so He condensed a lifetime of marital bliss into nineteen years because He wanted us to immensely enjoy each other while Vincent was here. When that thought came, I said, "God you don't owe me nothing; You've already given me more than I deserved. You're worthy to have what you want, and I'm thankful for what you gave us. It didn't seem right in my sight but even so Father, for so it seemed right in your sight."

Even knowing that, my prayer times were still filled with tears because I missed my husband so. I missed the tangible love that exuded from him towards me, the love that I could touch as it touched me. While we were teaching the marriage course, we wanted others to have what we had in our marriage, but it might not have been meant for everyone to have what we had; that might have just been our path. Not to say others are not happy in their marriages, but we knew that God had His finger on ours.

What I've come to realize is that when God breaks your heart, He knows how to mend it and use the brokenness for His glory because it is out of the broken places that true worship arises. My morning prayer times were necessary and most precious because it was in those time that I gave God all the sorrow I had because He had taken my husband. I not only took my sorrow to God but through all the tears, I let Him know that He was still worthy to have what He wanted even if it meant taking my husband from me. God did not get tired of me coming day after day with my broken heart. For those times when I felt like He owed me something, I didn't realize what He was giving me, which was more of Him. He was taking all the broken places and filling them with Himself.

It has been several years since Vincent has gone and when I look at his picture now, I don't say "Doggonit, you left me!" I know if he could have, he would have rather lived than died; but he accepted God's will for his life. I still have my moments when I tear up from missing him so much, especially when I am driving in the car alone and I hear a song that reminds me of us; but I am so thankful that I know my tears are not vain tears. God is always there to fill me with His strength and I know God's love does, God's love has, and God's love will continue to sustain me for His glory. He has proven to me that He is more than enough, even when I did not feel like He was. I will forever treasure the memories and the love He filled me with by way of Vincent Gerard Paige Sr.

CHERISHED MEMORIES

Me and Vincent hanging out at The Bar in the beginning of our relationship.

Before going to a holiday party at the company Vincent worked for, we took a picture in front of his Cadillac Seville. I was not a fan of that car.

I was seven months pregnant with Vincent Jr.

Vincent and Vincent Jr. about a month after his birth.

Vincent with the kids and our beloved dog Bear.

This was a birthday celebration for Delrick. Birthdays were always celebrated even if it was just us and a cake.

Our wedding was simply beautiful. Vincent said God blessed our marriage when the sun peeked through the clouds and shined on us. I'd say he was right about that.

Our wedding party included our kids, Geralyn, Victor and my nieces Jafaye and Shakira. Shakia is pictured in Vincent's family photograph on the next page. She's the one in her mother's arms.

Vincent and I both come from large families and they were well represented at our wedding. My mom and siblings (top). Vincent's mom, siblings and uncles (bottom).

We were excited about our new life in Christ and going to church was a big part of it. At that age, Vincent Jr. went with the flow but Delrick and Fantasy's faces could not hide the fact that it was a bit too much church for them (top and bottom left). The pastor of the church we joined, Paul Wright, was highly respected by Vincent and had a significant impact on his spiritual growth and maturity (bottom right).

Our relationships with our fathers became important to us so we made it a priority to visit them. Vincent is with his father on one of our trips to Rochester, NY (right), and with my father during a trip to see him in Dothan, AL (left).

Me with Vincent's father in Rochester, NY (left). Vincent is pictured here with his brother Terdaryle and his kids Marielle and Terdaryle Jr. Also pictured are Jody and his wife Pat. Whenever we went to Rochester, Vincent made it a priority to visit with them (right).

April 9, 2005, Delrick married his wife Tamika. Tamika, me and Delrick (top left). Vincent and Tamika's dad, Kanute, who we call Jay (top right). Me and Tamika's mom, Vernice. (above).

Delrick and Tamika quickly made us doting grandparents to three beautiful girls, Lauryn, Aniston and Morgan.

Miami was the spot when we wanted a quick getaway. Vincent and Victor (top left). Victor, Vincent, Fantasy, Vincent Jr. and Sibel (top right).

Delrick and Tamika joined us for one of our grown and sexy weekends in Miami.

Celebrations with his family were important to Vincent. We were at one of my mother-in-law's birthday celebrations with her children and grandchildren (top). Vincent's with some of his siblings for a Fourth of July celebration (bottom).

This was our road trip to see Vincent's father in Rochester when Richard and Teal joined us. We were at a restaurant owned by Teal's grandfather near Washington, DC.

After touring some of the sites in Washington, DC, we took a seat on the lawn for a much-needed break.

Here we are on our fifteenth-year wedding anniversary cruise. Vincent was preparing to ride the jet ski. I just hopped on to take a picture with him (left). While in Turks and Caicos, our tour guide stopped at a beautiful beach (right).

I had broken my arm about three weeks before taking this picture. We were at the wedding of one of the young couples from the church we attended.

I was a fan of Paula Deen's cooking show so while we were in Savannah, GA, on one of our road trips, we went to The Lady and Sons restaurant.

We danced the night away at my 50th birthday party.

Vincent and me with some of the other married couples on The Marriage Is Perfect cruise.

Christmas 2012 with our family at my mom's house.

Being Granddad was the highlight of Vincent's life. He adored his grandbabies. It was through these girls that I saw another facet of him. They brought out a softness in him that I had not seen until they came along, and I am so happy I got to see him being Granddad. Lauryn's first Christmas (top left). Aniston and Morgan with Vincent while he's wearing the mask his father gave me (top right). Vincent with the girls at Wet 'n Wild (bottom left). The girls and Vincent the night before his shoulder amputation (bottom right).

Fantasy's graduation day was a week before Vincent's arm amputation (left). Morgan's graduation from Pre-K was two weeks after Vincent's arm amputation (right

June 30, 2013, was my 52nd birthday. We went dancing to celebrate and that was the last birthday we celebrated together (left). On our many getaways to Miami, we often stopped by to visit Ronnie, Vincent's cousin who lives in Miami. This is Vincent with his sister Karen and cousin Ronnie at the Paige Family Reunion. (right).

Vincent said he would not be able to dance at Gail's birthday party but once we started, we didn't sit down (top left). At one of the events at Invacare, Vincent is showing off his moves with the hula hoop (top right). After Vincent's passing, Invacare had a planned softball game and his team wore shirts that read, "In Memory of Vincent" (bottom left). Invacare also selected an employee annually who exhibited Vincent's attributes in the workplace to receive the Vincent Paige Memorial Award (bottom right).